DULUTH

To the memory of
Archie C. Salyards
First, last, and always
a Duluthian

Several ships carried tourists on the St. Louis River to Fond du Lac. After serving in Duluth as an overnight lake passenger ship, the
Chicora was rebuilt in 1878. As a day steamer, she carried passengers to Fond du Lac from 1912 to 1919.
Courtesy, Duluth Public Library

DULUTH

An Illustrated History of the Zenith City

By

Glenn N. Sandvik

Pictorial Research by Virginia Hyvarinen

"Partners in Progress" by William O. Beck

Produced in Association with the St. Louis County Historical Society

Windsor Publications, Inc.

Woodland Hills, California

Windsor Publications, Inc.
History Books Division

Publisher: John M. Phillips
Editorial Director: Lissa Sanders
Administrative Coordinator: Katherine Cooper
Senior Picture Editor: Teri Davis Greenberg
Senior Corporate History Editor: Karen Story
National Sales Manager: Bill Belger
Marketing Director: Ellen Kettenbeil
Production Manager: James Burke
Design Director: Alexander D'Anca
Art Production Manager: Dee Cooper
Typesetting Manager: E. Beryl Myers

Staff for *Duluth, An Illustrated History of the Zenith City*
Editor: Pam Taylor
Picture Editors: Annette Igra, Susan Wells
Assistant Editor: Todd Ackerman
Editorial Assistants: Karen Holroyd, Judy Hunter, Patricia Dailey, Phyllis Gray
Sales Manager: Steve Allison
Sales Representatives: Bette Chinander, Merle Howard
Production Artists: Ellen Hazeltine, Colleen Maggart
Typographers: Shannon Mellies, Barbara Neiman
Proofreaders: Kaylene Ohman, Doris Malkin

Designer: John Fish

Library of Congress Cataloging in Publication Data

Sandvik, Glenn N., 1950-
    Duluth, an illustrated history of the Zenith City.

    "Produced in association with the St. Louis County
Historical Society."
    Bibliography: p. 125
    Includes index.
    1. Duluth (Minn.) — History. 2. Duluth (Minn.) —
Description. 3. Duluth (Minn.) — Industries.
I. Beck, William O. Partners in Progress. 1983. II. St.
Louis County Historical Society (Minn.) III. Title.
F614.D8S26   1983   977.8'66   82-50190
ISBN 0-89781-059-7

TABLE OF CONTENTS

Patrons   6

Introduction   7

One

Fur-Trading Post to a Fledgling City   8

Two

Between the Water and the Wilderness   18

Three

The Years of Promise   28

Four

The Epitome of Prosperity   40

Five

Days of Glorious Effort   58

Six

Pathways to the Future   70

Seven

Partners in Progress   97

Sources   125

Index   126

DULUTH PATRONS

Chicago architect Daniel Hudson Burnham, who led the "City Beautiful" movement, designed the St. Louis County Courthouse in 1907 and suggested plans for Duluth's Civic Center. The City Hall (right) built in 1928 was designed by Thomas J. Shefchik, and the Federal Building (left), built in 1930, was designed by a federal architectural team. Courtesy, Duluth Public Library

INTRODUCTION

Because of its location at the western end of Lake Superior and its proximity to the Minnesota lumber and iron mining regions, the historical development of the City of Duluth has been unusually rich and significant. In less than half a century, beginning in the 1850s, Duluth grew from a small wilderness outpost of a few hundred people into a modern transportation and commercial center serving a vast region across northern Michigan, Wisconsin, and North Dakota, as well as northeastern Minnesota.

Duluth has continued to be a commercial hub up to the present, but in recent years also has developed into an important medical, educational, cultural, and tourist center.

The history of Duluth has been well-documented in several books and articles published over the years, but there is always more to tell. Indeed, it is often said that each generation writes its own history.

This book is not a chronological history in the traditional sense, but it does cover the broad spectrum of events that shaped Duluth's rich heritage. It is a compelling and fascinating story that has been enhanced by the hundreds of historical photographs and other illustrations especially selected for this book. Many have never before been published.

The St. Louis County Historical Society is the book's local sponsor. We hope everyone who reads it not only enjoys it but also learns more about one of Minnesota's most historically significant cities.

Lawrence J. Sommer, Director
St. Louis County Historical Society
Duluth, Minnesota

Chapter One

1679-1855

FUR-TRADING POST TO A FLEDGLING CITY

Joseph G. Wilson may indeed have had heavenly reward for those hardy souls who had settled in the Lake Superior wilderness foremost in his heart, but he also had an earthly reward for himself in mind as winter swept down the great lake late in 1855. Wilson was a Presbyterian minister laboring in the frontier town of Superior City, Wisconsin at the far western tip of Lake Superior. Early settler George Nettleton had offered him two lots in a new community then taking root across the bay from Superior City in the recently opened Minnesota Territory. All he had to do to claim this prize was find a fitting name for the city which, at least according to his founders, was bound for greatness.

The Reverend Wilson—one of but a handful of early residents regarded as having scholarly or spiritual insights sufficient to make a future metropolis—sought counsel from his missionary predecessors. While reading an English translation of *The Jesuit Relations* (a collection of letters reporting the priests' activities to patrons in France), he came across the accounts of a minor French nobleman who traversed Lake Superior and left his footprints in the sand at the Head of the Lakes a century and three-quarters earlier in 1679. Wilson liked the character of the Frenchman as related by the missionary priests. And he liked the cadence of the Frenchman's name.

So Joseph Wilson offered the name of Daniel Greysolon, Sieur du Lhut to the men then platting the would-be Minnesota metropolis. The frontier entrepreneurs shared Wilson's enthusiasm for the royal-sounding title. The nobleman himself apparently spelled his name two different ways—*du Lhut* most

French explorer Daniel Greysolon, Sieur du Lhut, greets Dakota and Ojibway (Chippewa) Indians after landing on what is now Park Point in June 1679. This scene is depicted in a 1919 painting by C.C. Rosenkrantz, which hangs in the St. Louis County Historical Museum.

Alfred Merritt described the Superior area as it looked when he arrived in October 1856: "It was practically in a state of nature. The Indians were there with their wigwams scattered up and down Minnesota and Wisconsin points." The wigwams in this Chippewa camp were made with birch bark and rushes thrown over poles. Courtesy, Minnesota Historical Society

Beaver was the fur traders' prized catch. Its wooly underfur was valued most for making high-fashion felt hats. In 1760 the Hudson's Bay Company exported enough beaver pelts to England to make 576,000 hats. Photo by Bruce Ojard

often, but also *Duluth*—and the English preference was for the latter. Duluth has ever since been on the maps of the North American continent.

While du Lhut was not the first white man to travel on Lake Superior, it is generally acknowledged that he was the first to reach the western extremity of the Great Lakes. The first white man to travel on the lake is believed to have been Etienne Brule, who claimed to have seen Indian copper diggings on the lake in the early 1620s; the copper mines, or pits, had been dug for centuries by tribes unknown. By 1632 Samuel de Champlain, who had employed Brule as an agent and interpreter for his fur-trading enterprises in the American wilderness, had published a map which depicted some of the features of eastern Lake Superior.

Thus for half a century before du Lhut wintered at Sault Ste. Marie in 1678-1679, the *coureurs de bois* (literally, the "woods runners," a colorful breed of French and half-breed fur trappers) and Jesuit missionaries, traversed Superior's waters. The former went in search of fortunes in beaver pelts and rumored copper riches while the latter sought native souls for God's glory.

In the summer of 1678, du Lhut, in a spirit of adventure typical of young men of his wealth and station, set out to explore the American interior. De Lhut was a compatriot and trusted counsel of Count Frontenac, and traveled under his authority, in pursuit, perhaps, of the long-sought Northwest Passage, or an all-water route to the Pacific. Du Lhut himself proclaimed his voyage a peacemaking mission, as he sought to arrange for a truce among the warring Indian nations of the western Great Lakes and eastern Great Plains.

He particularly hoped to bring an end to years of bitter warfare between the Sioux (or Dakota) of the Upper Mississippi and the Chippewa (or Ojibway) of the western lakes. Because of that conflict, du Lhut wrote to his superiors in Montreal from his winter post at the Sault that neither Sioux nor Chippewa would hunt around the Head of the Lakes, an area "according to the savages, swarming with beaver."

In June 1679, du Lhut and his *voyageurs* beached their canoes on the spit of land now known as Minnesota Point. In the fall of that year, du Lhut met with the Indian nations at Fond du Lac, where, in his own words, he

arranged for the Asseniboins [Great Plains Indians of the Siouan linguistic stock] as well as all the other nations of the north to meet at the head of Lake Superior in order to make peace with the Dakota, their common enemy. They all did come, and I had the good fortune of gaining their esteem and friendship.

Daniel Greysolon, Sieur du Lhut

Daniel Greysolon, Sieur du Lhut, was perhaps typical of the lesser French aristocracy in the late 17th century. He was born in the village of Saint Germain-Laval in 1639 and, like many of his contemporaries, chose for himself a career in the army of King Louis XIV.

Du Lhut received a commission as a *gendarme de la garde du roi*—a royal guard of Louis XIV's court. But while the Sun King waged war across Europe, the young du Lhut grew restless with his routine courtly duties. He requested and was granted an appointment as a marine captain in New France. Some time in the early 1670s du Lhut migrated to Montreal, preceded there by a brother, an uncle, and two cousins, all of whom held government posts of import and influence. In Canada he lived the life of a gentry bachelor, carrying out his military obligations while still enjoying the social privileges to which his birth entitled him. He returned to France in 1674 but was back in Montreal that same autumn.

In 1678 du Lhut led a small party westward into the great American wilderness. Some historians suggest that he was spurred by unrequited love in the capital of New France, but du Lhut himself wrote that he left Montreal to make peace among the several Indian tribes that migrated and traded around Lake Superior. And, like many of his New World counterparts, he no doubt hoped to discover the Northwest Passage, that oft-rumored route to the Pacific and the Orient.

In the autumn of 1679 du Lhut succeeded in his first mission, convincing the Chippewa, Sioux and other tribes to recognize the authority of Louis XIV and to agree to cease their battles. The site of that historic parley was at the Head of the Lakes, in or near the city which now bears the Frenchman's name. Du Lhut's latter dream was never realized, as he went no farther west than the upper reaches of the Mississippi River.

In 1680 he mapped a trade route from Lake Superior to the Mississippi via the Brule and St. Croix rivers. Hearing reports that a large band of Sioux was holding a Jesuit priest hostage, du Lhut set off on an arduous journey and single-handedly "rescued" Father Louis Hennepin. (There remains some question, however, as to whether the missionary was a captive or merely a guest of the Indians.)

Returning to Montreal, du Lhut found that his motives for going west had been publicly questioned, and he felt it necessary to return to France to clear his name before his king. This he did in 1681 and returned to military duty in New France. For the next quarter century he commanded several French outposts around the Great Lakes and did battle against the English and their native allies.

But among the Indian nations friendly to France, du Lhut was generally both admired and respected for his firm yet fair dealings. For instance, in 1683, while du Lhut was in charge of the post at Mackinac, two French traders were murdered. He arrested three Indians accused of the crime and gave them a thorough and impartial trial, where all were found guilty.

Du Lhut immediately had two of the convicts executed in front of a predominantly Indian crowd while releasing the third to go free. This bold and decisive brand of justice sat well with the Indians, whose own views of retribution and punishment included "an eye for an eye." The action must certainly have bolstered du Lhut's reputation.

In 1707 Daniel Greysolon retired from the military and took up bachelor quarters in the home of a wealthy Montreal merchant. He died there on March 25, 1710, and was plainly yet eloquently eulogized by the governor of New France who wrote to the royal court in Paris: "Captain du Lhut died last winter. He was a very honest man."

This David Ericson painting depicts Daniel Greysolon, Sieur du Lhut, of the Royal Guard of Louis XIV in his home town of Saint Germain-Laval in about 1676. David Ericson was a Duluth artist who studied in New York, Belgium and France. Photo by Bruce Ojard

Although du Lhut did manage to arrange a fragile truce, the Lake Superior country remained basically unchanged for more than a century following his peacemaking tour. The Frenchman's treaty notwithstanding, the Chippewa and Sioux soon reverted to their bloody rivalries; the oral histories of both tribes, which have been handed down from generation to generation, reverberate with proud tales of murder and mayhem. Yet those histories also tell of the everyday concerns of the men and women who struggled for subsistence in this often harsh land.

The Chippewa came often to the Head of the Lakes. One or more bands encamped regularly near Fond du Lac, at the foot of the St. Louis River, in what is now the city of Duluth's most westerly neighborhood. They harvested fish from the rapids of the St. Louis and in season went to the sugar bush farther west to tap the abundant maple for its sweet sap. They followed the beaver, deer, moose, and elk throughout the woodlands. And once a year they traded with the whites, exchanging their pelts for steel traps, shoddy rifles, colorful blankets and—all too often—liquor. Naturally, there were always unscrupulous merchants and mercenaries, both white and half-breed, eager to take advantage of many of the natives' propensity for the substance.

The Hudson's Bay Company, the first great fur-trading enterprise of North America, may have had a minor post at Fond du Lac as early as 1692. But the principal trading post on Lake Superior was Grand Portage, some 150 miles northeast of the lakehead. This was the stepping-off point for the myriad inland waterways which led the French and their successors all the way down the Mississippi, as far west as the Rockies and to the tundra of northern Canada. Grand Portage truly was the hub of the fur-trading empires which made countless men rich and which outfitted the royalty and the dandies of Europe.

The next record of an outpost at the Head of the Lakes appears in about 1765, when the trader Alexander Henry dispatched agents from his trading headquarters at La Pointe in Lake Superior's Apostle Islands to barter for beaver with the Indians of Fond du Lac. It mattered little to the natives that, at least on paper, authority over their hunting grounds had by then passed from the French to the British with the defeat of the French in the Seven Years' (French and Indian) War. Nor did it matter much to the Indians, or to that odd lot of French Canadians and their mixed-blood offspring who for more than a century provided the real impetus of the fur trade, when the region passed, almost by default, to the control of the new and struggling government of the American republic.

This reconstruction of John Jacob Astor's Fond du Lac trading post was built in 1935, half a block south of the 1816 site on the St. Louis River. It was said that logs from the original American Fur Company post bearing the Astor stamp were used in the reconstruction. Courtesy, Duluth Public Library

Although the battles of the American Revolution had little direct effect on the people of the Lake Superior region, the land figured prominently in postwar territorial negotiations. It was, in fact, a cartographer's error which left the site of the city of Duluth within the territorial United States rather than in British Canada. When British and American negotiators gathered in Paris in April 1782 to officially put an end to the Revolutionary War, the rebels-turned-citizens were bold in their peace demands.

Chief American agent Benjamin Franklin at first insisted that the British surrender all of their North American holdings—including all of Canada and the West, as well as the former 13 colonies. The British countered by suggesting a northwest border to follow the Ohio River. The peace commissioners compromised on a line running through the center of the Great Lakes.

But in plotting this boundary through Lake Superior, the Paris negotiators relied on a map prepared by British cartographer John Mitchell in 1755. Mitchell's map, likely drawn solely from the

Charles Cadotte, who moved to Superior in 1852, was a lineal descendant of the famous "Grand Michael" Cadotte and his brother Jean Baptiste. In the late 18th century the Cadotte brothers ran the North West Company post, which was located at what is now the intersection of East Second and Winter Street in Superior, Wisconsin. Courtesy, Douglas County Historical Society

accounts of voyageurs, traders, and missionaries, contained many inaccuracies, chief among them the location of the headwaters of the great lake. Mitchell depicted Superior as flowing out of the Lake of the Woods via some nonexistent "Long Lake," actually the Pigeon River. This waterway, then—rather than the St. Louis River, which more closely represents the true center of the Great Lakes—became the international border. Thus Duluth and all of the Minnesota Arrowhead, with its vast mineral and timber riches, quite accidentally became the property of the United States.

About 1792 the French fur trader Jean Baptiste Cadotte, in the employ of Alexander Henry's North West Company, built a wood picket fort at the Head of the Lakes to carry on the fur trade with the Indians of the Fond du Lac district. Cadotte's post stood on the Wisconsin side of the St. Louis River near the confluence of that river and Lake Superior in the present city of Superior. The fort was destroyed by fire about 1800, by which time the entire region was generally recognized to be within the domain of the United States; however, the two strongest and most vigorous competitors in the peltry commerce remained the predominantly British-controlled Hudson's Bay Company and the predominantly French-controlled North West Company.

In 1809 the German-born American entrepreneur John Jacob Astor established a post at Fond du Lac, on the Minnesota side of the St. Louis River, for his newly-organized American Fur Company. He employed as his resident agent the trader William Morrison. However, the venture was apparently a financial failure, as the Chippewa continued to do most of their trading with their longtime French and English partners.

But Astor realized the value of the Lake Superior commerce and was eager to capture that commerce for himself. Following the War of 1812 he helped convince the United States Congress to pass a law specifically barring foreigners from trading in American territory—virtually assuring him a monopoly in the western lakes fur markets. Astor secured a firm hold on trade through the Upper Mississippi Valley, and ultimately the entire nation. He built a substantial new American Fur Company station at Fond du Lac in 1816-1817, and for the next three decades this settlement served as one of civilization's bastions in the Great Lakes wilderness.

Michigan territorial governor Lewis Cass, a man who devoted much of his time and considerable energies to exploring and opening the upper Great Lakes region, first visited Fond du Lac in 1820 while on an expedition to promote friendship between the federal government and the Indians of the region. He also sought to map the territory between Lake Superior and the Mississippi River and to assay that territory's natural resources. David Douglass Bates, Cass's topographer, kept a daily journal of the party's progress. On July 5 he wrote:

> About 1 o'clock arrived at the mouth of the St. Louis [River], which having entered, we bid a final adieu to Lake Superior . . . The first part of the St. Louis we found marshy, but afterwards the flats of the shore became more elevated and dry and present the appearance of rich river bottoms. As we approached the establishment [at Fond du Lac], these [flats] are covered with thickets of wild roses and a profusion of every hue and color.

The Cass party stayed but one night at the American Fur Company establishment, which was still in the charge of William Morrison, before climbing the nine miles up the Grand Portage of the St. Louis and heading westward toward the Mississippi.

Lewis Cass returned to Fond du Lac six years later to persuade the Lake Superior Chippewa to ratify a federal treaty which he had negotiated at Prairie du Chien the previous summer. That treaty established the supremacy of the United States government and attempted to stem the bloodshed among the Sioux, Chippewa and other Indian tribes by setting geographic boundaries between them. Thomas L. McKenney, who headed the agency he had named the "U.S. Indian Department," served as joint commissioner with Cass at Fond du Lac, and left perhaps the best description of the fur-trading post as it looked in 1826:

> The agents of [American Fur] company made a polite tender to us of the buildings, of which there were six or seven. They are of logs, one story high, and covered with bark; not their roofs only, but their sides and ends also. They stand on the north side of the river, and about thirty yards from it . . . The river at this place is not more than one hundred and fifty years wide, and in its middle, directly opposite the buildings, is a small oval island. On this are a good many Indian lodges . . . Between the buildings and the hill, on the north, is a piece of cleared ground, picketted in, for the growing of potatoes, and in the enclosure is a small patch of wheat, some of which is just beginning to head. In this enclosure, and near the hills, are two smaller enclosures—one, the larger, is the grave-yard for the whites, the traders; the smaller is for Indians.

On August 5, 1826, Cass McKenney, and the leaders of the sundry bands of Chippewa signed the Treaty of Fond du Lac. In addition to establishing tribal boundaries, the pact granted the federal government the right "to search for, and carry away, any metals or minerals" from the Chippewa territory. The Chippewa, in return, were given land guarantees of $2,000 per year (for the entire tribe), and were provided an Indian school at Sault Ste. Marie. The ceremony marking the signing of the treaty was concluded with the smoking of the peace pipe, the exchange of gifts, and some lofty political oratory from whites and Indians alike.

At the time of the treaty William Morrison remained the agent in charge of the American Fur Company's Fond du Lac post. Indeed, by the mid-1820s, he was factor at Fond du Lac, a title which enabled him to share in the company's profits with Astor and the other partners. By the early 1830s, William A. Aitkin had succeeded Morrison as factor, and Aitkin's must truly have been a profitable post.

In the summer of 1832, Henry Rowe Schoolcraft, Indian agent from Sault Ste. Marie, went with a small party on an expedition to the headwaters of the Mississippi. Passing through Fond du Lac, one of its members wrote that he "was not a little surprised to find four hundred souls, half breeds and white men." When Astor's original government charter expired in 1833, the Lake Superior portion of the fur company was reorganized under the leadership of fur trader Ramsay Crooks—it was at this time that the company was attempting to stabilize its financial fortunes by diversifying into the commercial fishing business at its Lake Superior stations.

Also by the 1830s a new generation of missionaries was entering western Lake Superior. Rather than the Catholic fathers, this new breed was predominantly Protestant. The Reverend W.T. Boutwell, who had accompanied Schoolcraft on his expedition, claimed he preached the first sermon in English at the Head of the Lakes in June 1832 to a congregation of about 40 whites; then, through an interpreter, he addressed a group of French half-breeds and Indians. Boutwell stayed on in the Lake Superior region doing missionary work for the next 15 years.

In 1833 the Reverend Boutwell was joined at Fond du Lac by a young man who had been dispatched by the American Board of Foreign Missions to educate the Chippewa of Lake Superior. For 12 years the young missionary, Edmund Franklin Ely, worked tirelessly under often miserable conditions to share his knowledge and his Christian faith with the Indians, all the while recording his observations on native life and death in a carefully preserved personal diary. "Could some of my dear friends have been here this morning they would indeed have felt themselves on heathen ground," he wrote on his first visit to Fond du Lac.

Ely traveled regularly between mission stations at Fond du Lac, Sandy Lake in north central Minnesota, and American Board of Foreign Missions' headquarters at La Pointe. In 1835 Ely and his new bride, Catherine Bissell of the Mackinac Mission, leased a parcel of land from the Indians at Fond du Lac where he built a mission school and quickly commenced grammar and arithmetic classes for the children near the post. He also taught catechism to Christian converts of all ages and organized a children's choir. And Ely worked diligently to compile a Chippewa dictionary so he could translate his song books and Bibles at the same time he taught his charges to read.

By the time the Elys left Fond du Lac in 1839 to run the Pokegama mission school, near Pokegama Falls in what is now Itasca County, the American Fur Company was falling on hard times. Fashionable Europeans now preferred silk hats to beaver ones, and as supplies of beaver pelts diminished, the demand for peltry became as depressed as the nation's economy, still suffering from the effects of the Panic of 1837. And while, into the early 1840s, the fur company's fisheries were reaping bountiful harvests from Lake Superior, the volume of fish sold didn't come close to

Lake Superior has supplied a treasure of fish to the restaurants of America. The 1886 catch was reported to be nearly two million pounds of assorted fish, with whitefish and trout as specialties. Courtesy, Duluth Public Library

the amount of fish harvested.

By 1842 the company had failed financially, and over the next several years its holders gradually liquidated their Lake Superior posts. The Fond du Lac fur station closed in 1847, dissolving the community as a year-round settlement, although the mission continued there until 1849. In that same year Reuben B. Carlton, who would be instrumental in the politics and settlement policies of the region, took up part-time residence at Fond du Lac as a federally subsidized farmer and blacksmith to the Indians. It was also in 1849 that Minnesota officially became a United States Territory.

In the 1840s a new industry arose in the Lake Superior wilderness—copper mining. This was not truly a new venture; it dated to antiquity. Ancient miners had chiseled pure copper from veins and outcroppings on Isle Royale and along the Keweenaw Peninsula some 12,000 years ago. Unknown tribes in succeeding ages continued to carry off Lake Superior copper, and articles made with this precious metal have been found throughout central North America and as far south as the ancient Mexican empires.

Indian tales of copper riches were whispered to the first Frenchmen who entered Superior. Jesuit Claude Allouez was dispatched to Lake Superior in 1665 to save Indian souls, but he was also directed by his Jesuit superiors, who were in close alliance with the French Court at this time, to search for copper. He

secured samples of native ore, probably from Isle Royale.

Nearly a half century later, in 1710, the intendant of New France was impressed enough by the continuing copper rumors to write his superiors in Paris that the Indians "claim that the Island Minong [Isle Royale] and small islets in the lake are entirely of copper." In 1767 fur trader Alexander Henry obtained a mineral license from the British Crown and sought unsuccessfully to open a mine in the vicinity of the Ontonagon Boulder, a several-hundred-ton specimen of pure copper buried along a South Shore stream which had long been held in reverence by the native tribes that populated the lake.

Nearly all white men who visited Superior in the early 19th century commented on copper signs and copper traces. In August 1826, Thomas McKenney noted that a party of federal agents had been sent back down the lake from Fond du Lac to try—once again unsuccessfully—to remove the Ontonagon Boulder. But it took the reports of Douglass Houghton, who mapped the Keweenaw in the late 1830s, to touch off a real copper rush. By the mid-1840s major copper mines were being worked by Eastern-financed mining companies along the Keweenaw and on Isle Royale. And many avaricious eyes looked longingly toward the American North Shore between Fond du Lac and the Pigeon River, a region from which whites were still excluded.

As early as 1846 some unknown speculators had attempted

to illegally open a copper mine near the mouth of the French River, just north of the current Duluth city limits. The venture lasted less than a year. Beginning in 1847 United States geologist Joseph G. Norwood conducted a minerological survey of the North Shore. His report, presented to Congress in 1852, gave substantial credence to the rumors of cupric riches and intensified the demands that the federal government open the Minnesota Arrowhead to white settlement. Norwood's report also noted the presence of extensive iron deposits in the region, but those statements were largely ignored.

In 1852 the federal government commissioned the first land survey at the Head of the Lakes. George R. Stuntz, a man whose name would become almost legendary in Duluth, ran the northern boundary between the state of Wisconsin and Minnesota Territory and subdivided several square miles on land on the eastern side of the St. Louis river and bay. In the summer of 1853 there was a land rush to claim the choicest parcels in a Wisconsin frontier townsite whose founders were confident business and industry would beat a path to their doorstep. One of those claiming 160 acres along the Wisconsin bayfront was the Reverned Ely. In early 1854, Superior City, Wisconsin was officially organized. Yet the adjacent Minnesota Territory remained open to Indians only.

There was, in addition to the rumors of copper fortunes to be found throughout the western Lake Superior region, another very sound economic reason why men headed for the Head of the Lakes in the early 1850s. Channels and locks were being carved out at Sault Ste. Marie which would allow large, deep-draft ships to sail all the way to the lakehead from such lower-lakes ports as Buffalo, Cleveland, Detroit, and Chicago. In fact, some of the promoters of Superior City were predicting their community would soon outstrip Chicago as the focal point for trade between America's westward-moving population and the established commercial centers of the East.

Congress, bowing to political pressures from men of influence and money in the Minnesota Territory, appropriated funds for construction of a military road from St. Paul to the tip of Lake Superior. Political lobbyists from Wisconsin flexed their muscle and had the road's northern terminus switched from Fond du Lac

The rapids ("sault") of the Sault Ste. Marie were first altered in the 1790s to facilitate fur trade traffic between Lake Superior and Lake Huron. In 1895 this large lock was built to meet the pressing needs of marine commerce, replacing the 1855 double-lift lock. Courtesy, Duluth Public Library

Signed at La Pointe with the Chippewas of Lake Superior and the Mississippi, the Treaty of 1854 ceded most of the Arrowhead Country to the U.S. government and created two reservations. The Indians received annually, over a 20-year period, $5,000 in coins, and $8,000 in goods. Courtesy, Minnesota Historical Society

to Superior City, although the condition of this 150-mile wilderness trail left most who traveled it moaning—"the worst road I have ever experienced"... "much of the way it was mud above our knees," wrote one Lake Superior pioneer. The old military road was for several years the only land route from the lakehead to the established communities and commercial centers to the south.

In the fall of 1854 federal agents once again called the Chippewa to treaty with the government. In mid-September some 5,000 Chippewa gathered at La Pointe in the Apostle Islands to consider the terms of a federal proposal for their tribe to surrender exclusive rights to the vast wilderness north and west of Lake Superior. After two weeks of haggling among themselves and with the government agents, aging Chief Buffalo and 84 other Chippewa headmen put their marks upon the Treaty of La Pointe.

Almost immediately, mineral prospectors and land speculators swarmed across the bay from Superior City, staking claims all along the Minnesota side of the St. Louis bay and river as well as down the North Shore nearly to Grand Portage. Within the next few years at least 11 townsites would be platted within the bounds of what is now the city of Duluth. A dozen or more would-be population centers would also be staked out along the shore between the lakehead and the Canadian border. Nearly all were founded on copper dreams, but many proved to be little more than "paper towns."

Surveyor George Stuntz is generally recognized as having been the first settler, and thus the premier citizen, of what is now Duluth. While mapping the Wisconsin-Minnesota boundary and the site of Superior City in 1852 and 1853, Stuntz hired three Indians to build a residence, warehouse, and dock for him near the entry to Superior Bay on Minnesota Point, that same spit of sand which Daniel Greysolon had crossed in 1679. The surveyor was also licensed to trade with the Indians, so there was nothing improper about establishing his home in the Chippewa territory. Stuntz, who up until that time had led a transient life in the American frontier, recalled 40 years later why he chose to settle where he did:

> I came in 1852. I saw the advantage of [Minnesota Point] as clearly then as I do now. On finishing the survey for the government, I went away to make a report, and returned the next spring and came for good. I saw as surely then as I do now that this was the heart of the continent commercially, and so I drove my stakes.

In addition to Stuntz and Reuben Carlton, Fond du Lac's resident blacksmith and farmer, perhaps the other earliest settler of Duluth was George E. Nettleton. He was, like Stuntz and Carlton, a licensed Indian trader. In the winter of 1853-1854 Nettleton built for himself and his family a log cabin trading post near the foot of Minnesota Point. Thus when the Treaty of La Pointe was signed in 1854 there were already at least three pioneers who had put down their roots on the site of Duluth.

There arose at this time, and for months and years following the opening of the Arrowhead, considerable rivalry between the people who planted their futures on the Wisconsin side of the St. Louis River and those who flocked to the Minnesota side, many of whom had settled at least temporarily in Superior City. A friendly community competition flourishes to this day.

Buffalo (Ke-che-waish-ke), the principal chief of the Lake Superior Chippewa, received one square mile of land in what is now downtown Duluth when he signed the Treaty of La Pointe in 1854. Thirty years later Frederick Prentice, a former Lake Superior trader, would cast a pall over the city's business development when he filed a series of lawsuits in federal court, trying to establish himself as the rightful holder of the "Buffalo claim." Courtesy, Minnesota Historical Society

George B. Sargent, who was Stuntz's immediate superior as federal surveyor-general for Iowa, Wisconsin, and Minnesota, also was an early investor in and promoter of the Head of the Lakes. In February 1855, while touring the East Coast to lecture on "the New West," Sargent prophesied to an audience in Boston: "At this point, at the mouth of the St. Louis River, will grow a great city, where Europe and Asia shall meet and shake hands. At this very point must center the trade of 20 American states yet unknown, and the British trade of the Red River settlements and of Hudson Bay."

Against this backdrop of history and boundless optimism for the future, George Nettleton petitioned the Reverend Joseph Wilson to name his new Lake Superior townsite. And although it is not recorded whether Wilson ever received his promised property reward, he is remembered to this day for putting Duluth on the map.

Chapter Two

1856-1868

BETWEEN THE WATER AND THE WILDERNESS

"We were all rich in anticipation, and we were all going to be perfectly happy."

Thus did George Nettleton's wife summarize the emotions and expectations of many who were investing their money and their energies to develop Duluth and the score of other townsites stretched out along Lake Superior's North Shore in 1856. At that time, and for several years to come, individual energy was far more abundant at the Head of the Lakes than monetary wealth. Anticipation made few pioneer Duluthians rich, but it did provide a rich foundation for the community's eventual prosperity.

George Stuntz's trading post/warehouse near the tip of Minnesota Point was one of several centers of commerce and habitation which took root in Minnesota immediately following the Treaty of La Pointe. Stuntz warehoused food, furniture, building supplies, and fuel, as well as his own surveying and sawmill equipment; there the Indians bartered for food and domestic supplies, as did some of the early settlers of Superior City. In addition to trading with the Chippewa, whose encampments often surrounded his on the promontory, Stuntz held a near-monopoly in the transfer business. From his dock he ferried cargo and passengers in flat-bottomed mackinaw boats across the shallow backwater bay to Superior and to the Minnesota settlements. Unlike many of his contemporaries, Stuntz never bothered seeking townsite status for his home site.

Since the region depended almost entirely on marine traffic to deliver its lifeblood of food and commerce, Congress appropriated $15,000 in March 1855 for construction of a lighthouse at the

The oldest structure in Duluth, the Minnesota Point lighthouse was built in 1855 near the Superior entry. In 1878 the lighthouse was decommissioned and the lens, which was made by Bardon of Paris, was moved from the old tower to a new location on the west entrance to Superior Harbor. Courtesy, Duluth Public Library

Lewis Merritt from Ashtabula, Ohio, brought his family to Oneota ("the rock from which the people sprung") in 1856. Merritt left his sons this prophecy about Minnesota: "Some day there will be great mines there worth more than all the gold in California." Courtesy, Northeast Minnesota Historical Society

entry to Superior City. Captain R.G. Coburn of Superior was awarded the contract to build a light tower, adjacent keeper's dwelling, and two wooden piers to mark the harbor entry. He selected a location for the beacon almost in George Stuntz's backyard, a spot which had been identified as the "zero point" for lake charts by Lieutenant Henry Woolsey Bayfield of the British Royal Navy in 1823. (By establishing the base point for Lake Superior maps at the mouth of the St. Louis River, Bayfield apparently hoped to persuade American and British diplomats to move the U.S.-Canadian border there from the Pigeon River. His hopes were, of course, never realized.)

Coburn centered the tubular light tower, which stands to this day, over Bayfield's zero point. And the beacon proved to be a boon for the communities on both the Wisconsin and Minnesota sides of the lakehead; it also helped establish at an early date—at least from a maritime perspective—the oneness of the communities of the Head of the Lakes.

R.H. Barrett was employed as the first keeper of this light. For seven to eight months a year, as long as ice didn't stop traffic, he (and his successors) kept the kerosene lantern burning. When fog, a common condition, blanketed the Superior shorelines, the keepers activated a voice-powered fog signal, shouting through a tin bullhorn until their warnings were acknowledged from the decks of approaching vessels. And with the opening of the Soo Locks in 1855, each year brought an ever-larger number of sailing craft and steamships to the far end of the Great Lakes.

While the lighthouse was being built, five miles to the north, where the sandy point meets the pine-covered diabase hills, George Nettleton and several others staked out townsites which would eventually constitute the commercial heart of Duluth. But in 1856, not even the handful of people living there were as confident about the townsites' future as Nettleton. Even his wife later recalled, "I thought he had a pretty long head to see that there was going to be a city here sometime when there was then nothing— just a pile of rocks."

In addition to Nettleton's Duluth, neighboring townsites included North Duluth, platted by his brother William; Portland, on the lakeshore immediately north and east of Minnesota Point; and Cowell's Addition to Duluth, under the proprietorship of William G. Cowell.

Cowell was, like many of his counterparts, a promoter who invested in more than one of the early North Shore locations. In 1856 he surveyed a town he named Buchanan on 315 acres just west of the mouth of the Knife River. Calling on political cronies in the incoming administration of President-elect James Buchanan, Cowell sought and won for his townsite designation as the federal land office for northeastern Minnesota.

For the next three years anyone having property dealings with the federal government had to travel, almost always by boat, to Buchanan, remembered by one Duluth pioneer as "a pretty little city . . . at that time the emporium of the North Shore, with a pretentious hotel . . . the U.S. land office, steamboat docks, several saloons, boarding houses and so forth." But when the land office was transplanted to Portland in June 1859 because more people had settled at the Head of the Lakes then at Knife River, Buchanan quickly reverted to forest.

In Portland, where as early as 1856 the town fathers had tried to annex Nettleton's Duluth, the center of civic and commercial affairs was Sidney Luce's waterfront warehouse near what is now the foot of Second Avenue East. Luce had come to the Head of the Lakes from Ohio, seeking his fortune on a new frontier. In 1857 Luce, by his own admission "not well versed in western wildcat ways," had been persuaded by some of his fellow frontiersmen to erect a storehouse "in dimension thirty by forty feet, three stories high and garret above. The foundation was partly made by excavation of rock on the bank of the lake and partly by cribwork in the lake." One room was given over for such public uses as a post office, land office and county government headquarters as well as for public and private gatherings. There Luce conducted his business and held various public posts for both federal and local governments. Luce and his family also lived in the rough-hewn structure where

Edmund F. Ely

The oft-tested strength of his Christian spirit usually overrode the frail physical health of Edmund Franklin Ely, a pioneering soul who left his mark upon the Head of the Lakes both before and after the formal founding of Duluth. Ely was born in Wilbraham, Massachusetts, on August 3, 1809, and spent his youth and early adulthood preparing for a career in gospel ministry. In 1832 he accepted an assignment from the American Board of Foreign Missions to be an assistant instructor in its Lake Superior mission fields.

The Yankee minister/teacher kept a diary, which offers stark testimony about the life of its author and about life on America's northern frontier in the middle third of the 19th century. It also reveals a tireless devotion, despite persistent bodily infirmities, to the spiritual, mental, and physical well-being of his Ojibway charges.

In August 1835 Ely was married at La Pointe to Catherine Bissell, a mixed-blood graduate of the American Board's school at Mackinac Island. She worked beside Ely in the mission schools and bore and raised seven children in the Lake Superior wilderness.

Ely's New England stubbornness may have fortified his personal resolve, but it also was a pox upon many with whom he associated. He regularly bickered with the French Canadian overseers of the American Fur Company's Fond du Lac station for their adherence to Catholicism. He badgered and berated the traders and federal agents who allowed alcohol—"this bane of life," Ely termed it—to flow freely to the Ojibway. And while he

Edmund F. Ely

George R. Stuntz

George Riley Stuntz was an inveterate dreamer. He was, to be sure, many other things as well—surveyor and scientist, trader and timberman, mineral prospector and railroad promoter. And through all of these he was a maker of millionaires. But he was, above all else, a chaser of dreams.

Stuntz was born in Erie County, Pennsylvania, on December 12, 1820, the son of a Methodist clergyman and grandson of a Hessian soldier. He was educated in that state's common schools and entered Ohio's Grand River Institute.

His transient occupations brought him to western Lake Superior in 1852 to conduct land surveys for the federal government. Stuntz saw the harsh beauty of the Superior country and foresaw a great future for those who would temper that harshness; he settled for good in what would become Duluth. And through good times and bad he stayed, laboring always to make the lakehead the commercial, agricultural, and industrial hub of the Midwest.

By 1869 Stuntz had enlisted in the lobby to persuade Jay Cooke to invest in Duluth. In 1870 he platted the path of the continent-spanning Northern Pacific Railroad across Minnesota. About this time he also became allied with George C. Stone, a pioneer Duluth banker who had visions of profiteering on the Arrowhead's iron stores. In 1875 Stuntz guided a party of geologists, bankrolled by Philadelphia financier and industrialist Charlemagne Tower,

displayed the greatest compassion for the Indians, he nonetheless regularly upbraided them for their beggarly habits.

Tension between Ely and the natives at Fond du Lac mounted in 1838. "Scarcely a day passes that the Indians do not show their hatred and opposition in words concerning our residence here," he wrote that June. Yet Ely also gave voice to the reasons for the Indians' hostility, quoting a mixed-blood servant who had worked for the Ely family:

> Do you know why the traders treat us so? Perhaps they want us to die. We are poor, we have very few things. The traders want us to pay for everything. See all this land they have spoiled? What if we asked pay for everything? They have spoiled our things and they [the traders] must now pay for everything they have.

In 1841, while stationed at Pokegama, the Elys witnessed a Dakota attack upon the Ojibways in which two young girls were savagely dismembered. The incident marked yet another outbreak of generations of tribal hostilities and more than two decades of native violence in Minnesota.

In 1856 Ely moved his family across St. Louis Bay to Oneota. There he worked almost as tirelessly to promote the business and industrial interests of the townsite as he had in sharing his faith with the previous generation of lakehead residents. He and

George R. Stuntz

Catherine left Duluth for good in 1862 in the hope of aiding both his and his wife's frail health in more temperate California climates. There Edmund Ely died at age 83 in Santa Rosa.

across the western Mesabi hills and to the Vermilion fields. There he assayed ore at 63 percent iron and proclaimed it, "a magnificent sight." His proclamation went unheeded.

In 1881 he conducted a survey for Tower's iron railroad from Lake Vermilion to Agate Bay on Lake Superior and was one of the original partners in the Minnesota Iron Company, the first commercially successful mining operation in the state. But instead of claiming a percentage of the profits he opted for a standard surveyor's fee of $8 per day.

Then the pioneer-explorer retired and watched contentedly from Duluth as his dreams of regional greatness came true. A lifelong bachelor, he remained active in civic and social affairs, serving for nearly two decades as St. Louis County surveyor and as head of the St. Louis County Agricultural Society. Stuntz also took a scholarly turn, becoming an author and lecturer and advancing a theory that his home region had once been populated by a highly-skilled people who had mined and carried away fortunes in minerals.

Stuntz never did realize a just share of the immense wealth he helped uncover between Duluth and the Canadian border. He made others millionaires, but not himself. On October 24, 1902, George Riley Stuntz, the Zenith City's pioneer citizen, died in a charity hospital and was buried in a pauper's grave on a wind-swept hillside in the city of his dreams.

Early settlers went to Minnesota Point to observe Indian ceremonies. An infant in this tikinagan, or cradle board, with its elaborate beadwork trim, dozes by one such gathering in 1870. Courtesy, Northeast Minnesota Historical Center

coarse boards were used for temporary third floor, packing boxes used in the shipment of household goods for partitions and cupboards, with stove pipe leading out of the window and without doors . . . Activity in building above, beneath and around soon made us comfortable, and upon this floor we lived twelve years in peace and Plenty, finally ending in prosperity.

Another township in what is now Duluth was Rice's Point, established by Orrin Rice on the peninsula of a swampy meadow which became the railroad and grain-shipping hub of the city. Rice, whose brothers Edmund and Henry were prominent in political affairs in St. Paul and all of Minnesota Territory, sought to have his townsite—temporarily renamed Port Byron to add a touch of glamor—made the seat of government for St. Louis County. Although this bid failed, the proprietor was granted a lucrative plumb when the Territorial Legislature gave him the exclusive right for 15 years to operate a freight and ferry service between Rice's Point, Minnesota Point and Connor's Point in Superior.

Next up the St. Louis River was Oneota, platted in 1856 by H.W. Wheeler, a sawmill operator from St. Paul, and first settled by Edmund Ely and his family. Other early settlers included Lewis and Hephzibah Merritt, whose brood of sons and grandsons could oversee the opening of Minnesota's treasurehouse of iron, and the Reverend James Peet. Peet, like Ely, kept a diary, a tome which contained a census for Oneota in the summer of 1856: "The town or city of Oneota contains about 20 inhabitants, three buildings, three huts for workshops and a store, a dock and a steam sawmill." The mill belonged to the Oneota Lumber Company, whose manager and principal stockholder was Edmund Ely.

Other townsites settled in what is now Duluth between 1855 and 1858 included Fond du Lac—where Reuben B. Carlton and at least two heirs to the factors of the American Fur Company were

proprietors—Middleton, Endion, Belville, and Fremont. When Minnesota became the thirty-fourth state of the union in 1857, among the first acts of the state legislature was to bestow official recognition upon nearly all these townsites. Most would retain their corporate autonomy for the next dozen years or more.

Also in 1857, the Minnesota Legislature authorized formation of the Minnesota Point Ship Canal Company. Among principals in the corporation, which was empowered to "cut a canal through Minnesota Point 300 feet wide," were George Nettleton and Edmund Ely. Although no canal would be dug for more than a decade, the fact that the legislature authorized such a project again illustrated just how vital marine commerce was to the people then settling the Minnesota Arrowhead.

Discounting the old military road—and all who were forced to travel that overland route were only too eager to discount and discredit it—Lake Superior provided the only entrance to the region. A bevy of small sailing vessels and steamships irregularly but frequently called at the lakehead, bringing more pioneers, their possessions, and provisions for those already in residence. Such workhorse packet steamers as the *Lady Elgin,* the *City of Superior,* and the *North Star* were always welcome callers. At times their calls took on life-and-death significance.

For instance, when James Peet arrived at Superior City via the military road in February 1856 he immediately recorded that there was "a scarcity of provisions and everything else but wood." In the fall of 1855, the last boats of the season had brought in more people than supplies, and insufficient stores were laid in. By March 31, his diary noted that "provisions are getting scarce here. It is feared that there will not be enough in the place to last until navigation opens. I learn that some 20 to 40 men have left the place because of a scarcity of provisions, and more are going soon."

The famine continued until May 9, when Peet wrote that "at 5:30 p.m. a steamboat made its arrival . . . she was hailed with cheers and shouts of joy by the citizens." The following autumn Peet noted with some reservation the arrival of winter supplies on October 9: "The 'Lady Elgin' came in; brought heavy cargo of provisions and enough whiskey to keep the whole town drunk all winter."

Such occurrences as season-long intoxication and winter deprivation served to show just how isolated the Lake Superior frontier was from the rest of the nation. And even among the townsites themselves the citizens were painfully aware of their remoteness. Mrs. Nettleton recalled a visit she and her husband had received from the Orrin Rices in 1855: "When the Rices had been there [on Rice's Point] for about four weeks, they came to visit us and Mrs. Rice said, 'Ladies, I didn't bring any work for it has been so long since I have seen the face of a white woman I just want to sit and look at you all awhile.'"

However, a few instances of refinement were visible. Several of the pioneers had extensive and admirable personal libraries. Edmund Ely even had a pipe organ built into his Oneota home for himself and his family. Yet for any who stayed any length of time, the most memorable of events may well have been the seemingly endless days, weeks and months of the most demanding physical labor.

While countless North Shore settlers—most of whom had come in contingents from New York, Pennsylvania, Ohio, and Michigan—toiled without success for the rumored copper riches, others were quick to capitalize on a resource which involved no prospecting—timber. By 1857 there were perhaps a dozen sawmills in operation between Fond du Lac and Pigeon River; most of them were, according to the federal agents at Buchanan, harvesting timber illegally from government land. In Duluth there were, in addition to Ely's mill in Oneota, a steam mill owned by George Nettleton and Joshua B. Culver on Lake Avenue near the present site of the Ship Canal, a combination wood mill and grist mill operated by Henry C. Ford in Milford about a mile upstream from Oneota, and one or more small sawmills on Rice's Point.

Each of the sundry townsites elected its own government officials. In some instances, nearly the entire population of a community was thus called to public office; in others, men held office in two or more towns at the same time. The first state election was held in 1857. Sidney Luce, then a newcomer to Duluth, found the Democrats in firm control and the democratic underpinnings of the election process sorely strained. He recalled:

There did not appear to be any organized opposition to the Democratic party, consequently election laws were construed to meet the emergencies of the candidates for office. Neighboring towns were well supplied with a migratory population, ready to respond to calls for assistance. An old coat and hat served [the purpose] of habilitating the Indian, rendering him a fully-fledged voter. Not being in the territory long enough to be entitled to vote, I was an idle spectator observing the farce being enacted.

The following year Luce was more than a spectator at another show of frontier electoral absurdity. As he later recalled, he was a county elections judge in November 1858 when the judges decided not to allow a group of foreign-born squatters to cast their ballots and the men denied ballots cast stones instead of votes. Said Luce,

the refusal to receive their votes resulted in disorder and rioting. The election was held on Minnesota Point, where stones were plenty, and they were freely used. Windows were smashed freely. During the melee one of the judges, L.H. Merritt, seized the ballot box and, with the loss of his hat, made away within safety. Fortunately, no one was seriously hurt, and still more fortunately it proved a wholesome lesson in subsequent elections.

Yet amid the farce and the absurdity the pioneers did manage to elect public officers who were on the whole conscientious and committed to their communities' betterment. State officials chosen in 1857 included W.W. Kingsbury of Endion as representative to Congress, Reuben B. Carlton of Fond du Lac as state senator and John Watrous of Buchanan as state representative. The original slate of St. Louis County officers was: Joshua Culver, clerk of district court; J.B. Ellis, sheriff; R.H. Barrett, register of deeds; Edwin Brown, auditor, and C.E. Martin, Vose Palmer, and Zack Brown, county commissioners. In 1856 Edmund Ely was named the county's first federal postmaster at Oneota; in 1857 Culver was appointed postmaster in Duluth. Another "first" worthy of note was the opening of the first public school in what is now Duluth at Oneota in the winter of 1856-1857. Jerome Merritt instructed about a dozen young scholars, including four of his brothers.

But just when it appeared that the fledgling Lake Superior

During the 1860s and 1870s, only a trail connected settlements such as Portland, Duluth, Oneota, and Fond du Lac. Travel was slow and difficult by land or by river route through a marsh that skirted the St. Louis Bay. Courtesy, Duluth Public Library

Development of the Vermilion Range and the Duluth and Iron Range Railroad created the shipping port of Two Harbors, shown here during construction of the ore docks in 1884. The town's name came from the existence of two bays there. Courtesy, Minnesota Historical Society

communities had taken root and would blossom between the water and the rocky-piney wilderness, an economic crisis gripped the nation. In the summer of 1857 the supply of money in the United States seemed to vanish. Currency, which had always been scarce in the frontier, became almost nonexistent. In the latter days of 1857 and into 1858, would-be mineral magnates, timber barons, and merchants simply left the Head of the Lakes region.

James Bardon, early historian and lifelong resident of Superior, summarized the situation nearly half a century later: "The sudden panic of 1857 was so chilling that the population speedily diminished about three-fourths . . . The lake steamers were overcrowded carrying people away, and the military road to St. Paul had more south-bound pedestrians than Coxey's army ever numbered." Among those joining the exodus was George Nettleton.

Buildings, indeed entire townsites, stood abandoned all along the North Shore. For those who stayed, the national depression gave a deeper meaning to hardships and hard times. In December 1857, for example, Edmund Ely had to dun the stockholders of the Oneota Lumber Company to cover the debts of his community: "You are hereby notified that an assessment of $2,784 on one

Both Nettleton brothers, William (left) and George, were involved in the early settlement of Superior, Wisconsin. They arrived from Ashtabula, Ohio, in 1853 on a sailing sloop and their names were among the first entries at the land office when it opened up the North Shore by Knife River. The brothers had left the area by 1869, but their name remains on an elementary school. Courtesy, Northeast Minnesota Historical Center

share in the townsite of Oneota has been made, said assessment to be applied to liquidating the liabilities incurred for the benefit of said townsite . . . in the election of mills, pier, boarding houses, buildings and other improvements." It is not recorded how much of this debt Ely was able to recapture before leaving the Head of the Lakes for good in 1862.

For those who didn't leave, fish and potatoes became the staples of their diets. Yet, perhaps because of the state of universal poverty, those who stayed banded even closer together. As Alfred Merritt would recall 60 years later: "In those early days we were all neighbors, from Beaver Bay down the North Shore to Fond du Lac and over into Superior. One cannot write about just one side of the state line, for in sickness and in joy there was no state line."

In 1860 fire destroyed the new federal land office at Portland and caused federal land business to be moved to a building owned by William Nettleton and Joshua Culver at the foot of Minnesota Point. It was eventually relocated to Sidney Luce's warehouse.

Also in 1859 a brewery was constructed in Portland. As Luce remembered it:

The season of 1859 was like its predecessor. There was nothing doing to relieve the stringency of the times. Our population was steadily decreasing, and to retain what remained was a matter of anxiety. In canvassing the matter, it was found that there were four single men out of employment, one of them being a practical brewer. He suggested the building of a brewery, as the four could do all the construction and carry it on. As this seemed likely to add a little to our enlivement, I encouraged the project by giving them a location . . . on what was then called Washington Avenue, on a small stream . . . The enterprise was not a pecuniary success.

It may not have succeeded at first, but for more than a century following the stringent times there was a successful brewery operation near the same location on what is now East Superior Street.

The federal census of 1860 counted 406 persons residing in all of St. Louis County; a sizeable number of that population is believed to have been Indians. In the spring of that year a new political force, the Republican Party, arose at the Head of the Lakes. James Peet's diary tells of several meetings of the "Republican

club" held at Oneota. Slavery, and general opposition to that American institution, was the principal concern at most of these gatherings.

Also in 1860, General George Meade, who would soon distinguish himself in the Civil War, joined other members of the Army Corps of Engineers encamped on Minnesota Point to survey the headwaters of Lake Superior. This survey of the Twin Ports harbor marked the first federal recognition of the need for improvements here, but Meade's survey was cut short by the outbreak of the Civil War, a conflict which further diminished the population of Duluth. Judge John R. Carey, a lifelong resident, recalled this flight: "During the summer of 1861 many departed, some with a patriotic spirit to their old homes in other states, and others to their old homes in Canada, where they would be safe from the draft."

Yet while the exodus continued well into the 1860s, there were also those who came to make their homes at the lakehead at this time. Among then was Luke Marvin of St. Paul, one of the absentee owners of the Oneota Lumber Company who moved his family north in 1861 to take charge of his investments. Years later his son wrote of the family's first impressions:

> After reaching Superior, we were ferried across the river to Duluth, which contained 10 or 12 families huddled about the base of Minnesota Point . . . The hills on which Duluth is now situated were then thickly covered with timber, there were no roads or streets, and the tents or shacks of the Indians were scattered all over the hills and Minnesota Point. The largest building in the place was Sidney Luce's warehouse.

Luce was involved in a brief revival of copper fever in Duluth in 1864 when he was employed to oversee the reopening of two mines of a company whose stockholders included Reuben B. Carlton. He wrote:

> The mines were one near Buchanan, the other one was called French River, about 15 miles from Duluth. Under the supervision of Mr. [Frank] Salisbury, considerable money was spent. The time of working . . . was about a year. The results proving unsatisfactory, work was suspended.

Late in 1865, Judge Carey decided to move his family from Oneota to Duluth. He later wrote:

> At this time, Duluth was almost entirely deserted; only two small houses . . . were occupied. The writer [Carey] had the freedom of the city and all the empty houses in it; he needed no key or burglar tools to enter them. He chose the Jefferson house, which was the most commodious and in the best repair.

(Carey apparently continued at this time to draw the distinction between Duluth and Portland, where Sidney Luce and others still resided.)

Then, in the winter of 1865-1866, a new mineral rush started the Duluth townsites on the road to revival. The previous summer, state geologist H.H. Eames had mapped the hills surrounding Lake Vermilion in far northern St. Louis County where he detected vast storehouses of hematite iron. But Eames had his heart set on finding a more precious ore, purportedly telling one of his assistants while standing atop a 50-foot iron outcropping. "To hell with iron ore! It's gold we're after!" And gold he found, or at least his survey report implied that there was gold to be found in abundance in the Arrowhead hillsides. That winter a gold rush was on to the Vermil-

Chippewas Joseph Northrup, Angeline Peterson Northrup, and their daughter Julia, were part of the Fond du Lac band and descended from the Indians who lived around the Fond du Lac post. The Treaty of 1854 created the Fond du Lac Reservation, 20 miles from Duluth, where the Northrup family resided. Courtesy, Minnesota Historical Society

ion fields, and all those rushing there had to pass through Duluth. Among the first to head north were George R. Stuntz and Lewis H. Merritt.

Stuntz and Merritt soon returned from Vermilion without fortunes in gold, but both brought back to the Head of the Lakes firm convictions that iron ore would be part of their home's rich destiny. Failing as a prospector, Stuntz went back to the work he knew best—surveying—and contracted with the federal government to chart and clear a road from Lake Superior to the gold fields. The Vermilion Trail which he cut for 60 miles over the rocks and through the swamps of northeastern Minnesota served first to give the Vermilion miners speedy exit from the wilderness when the gold rush fizzled; a decade and more later the route carried men and machines alike to carve iron from the Vermilion range.

Also in the years immediately following the Civil War another kind of rush—a railroad rush—was adding promises of prosperity to the townsites around Duluth. In 1861 the Minnesota Legislature had chartered the Lake Superior and Mississippi River Railroad and authorized swamp land grants totaling nearly 694,000 acres for the line to build a rail route from St. Paul to the Head of the Lakes. In 1864 Congress sweetened the pot considerably, offering a federal land grant of 960,000 acres for completion of the Lake Superior and Mississippi. The railroad's promoters planned to develop townsites along its route and hoped to turn Duluth into a major grain transshipment terminal.

As early as 1866 Philadelphia financier Jay Cooke had shown an interest in the Lake Superior and Mississippi and its vast land holdings. In June 1868 he visited Duluth to assess the potential of the railroad and its property. He conferred with some of those who had recently devoted their lives to the region—John Carey, Joshua Culver, Sidney Luce and Luke Marvin included—and returned East where that fall he decided to help float the bonds necessary to complete the rail line. Overnight, the Lake Superior and Mississippi, as well as the settlements at Duluth, skyrocketed to national prominence.

Officials in Superior and their financial backers had lobbied long and hard in St. Paul and Washington to locate the road's northern terminus in their Wisconsin community. But the Minne-

The India plied the waters between Buffalo and Duluth until 1892, transporting immigrants, building materials, and food to the West. Outgoing cargoes often also included buffalo hides. Duluth's first Catholic church, which stood on the site of the present day Sacred Heart Church, is visible in the left background. Courtesy, Northeast Minnesota Historical Center

In 1869, railroad engineers at Camp Number One worked on the Lake Superior and Mississippi Railroad, which linked Duluth with St. Paul. When the first passenger train arrived in Duluth on August 1, 1870, the whole town turned out to celebrate. The 154-mile trip took 16 hours and 20 minutes. Courtesy, Northeast Minnesota Historical Center

sota interests prevailed, and in the words of state representative James J. Egan, who first visited Duluth in May 1869:

> The lifeless corpse of Duluth . . . touched by the wand of Jay Cooke, sprang full-armed from the tomb; Banning, Branch and James Smith Jr. [executives of the Lake Superior and Mississippi and promoters of an all Minnesota railroad] had won the good fight and henceforth the sun of prosperity gilded the lake, and your bluffs echoed and re-echoed back the glad acclaim: "Minnesota has triumphed!"

George Stuntz had shared in the triumph by helping to lobby Jay Cooke through his old federal surveying supervisor and Cooke's New York business associate, George B. Sargent. But Stuntz nonetheless felt his home region was shortchanged by the manner in which the road was built. He wrote:

> The permanent growth of Duluth commenced in 1867 and 1868 with the construction of the railroad . . . Strangers began to look this way for investments, and to look up sites for business. St. Paul gave the company a bonus in city bonds of $250,000 and started the location and construction at that city. This was in violation of the charter, which said the company was to begin at Lake Superior . . . This was a setback of three years to Duluth, and the Lake Superior end lost the benefit of having expended two or three millions of dollars on the construction of this line.

Yet prosperity truly was riding the rails to Duluth. On July 4,

1868, Thomas Preston Foster, a part-time physician, part-time journalist, and full-time political partisan then practicing Republican politics and journalism in St. Paul, delivered a stirring visionary speech to what he termed "a straggling few" at a community celebration on Minnesota Point. He told his audience:

> It would not be remiss to dwell mentally for a while upon the future of this region, which is even now looming up in the near distance, promising to pierce and lighten up these forests with railways and farm homesteads, to mine these rocks into material wealth, to whiten yon huge sea with clouds of canvas, or fret it with volumes of propelling steam, to cover the shores of these broad calm bays with mast-studded wharves and monster grain warehouses, and to erect within the sound of the surge of Superior's waves a great city, which shall be the abode of commerce and manufactures and refinement and civilization, here nearly midway between the two main oceans of the world.

Foster extolled the virtues of the Lake Superior and Mississippi and other railways which he predicted would eventually stretch out from Duluth "almost up to the Rocky Mountain plains, which will yet be colonized and settled—the trade of which distant regions . . . will have been turned, as being the cheapest and most expeditious route, into the streets and avenues of our Zenith City of the Unsalted Seas."

The Zenith City of the Unsalted Seas . . . Thomas Foster's lofty laurel has ever since been a proud part of Duluth's history and heritage.

Chapter
Three

1869-1888

THE YEARS OF
PROMISE

By 1869 Duluth was quickly gaining quite a reputation . . . it was gaining a reputation as Jay Cooke's town. The Philadelphia financier's investment in the Lake Superior and Mississippi Railroad and in its allied land development companies ushered in a new era of population growth and prosperity for the Head of the Lakes. One of those new arrivals—they would later proudly refer to themselves as "'69ers"—counted only 14 families in Duluth in January 1869, but "by the Fourth of July 1869 there were 3,500 people in the place and still they were coming."

Luke Marvin would recall:

> This rush of people comprised all classes. Most of them were from Eastern states. Some came to work on the railroad; some came to engage in business; others . . . in lumbering, or to work in the woods as lumbering was then beginning to be a very important business, the railroads alone being great consumers of all kinds of timber for construction purposes.

Included in the rush was Thomas Preston Foster. Foster, the physician-politician who as editor of the *St. Paul Minnesotian* had extolled the Zenith City, was persuaded to establish the first newspaper in Duluth. In the spring of 1869 he had his press and typesetting equipment hauled overland from St. Paul, set it up in an abandoned barn near what is now Lake Avenue and Superior Street and on April 24 published the first edition of the weekly *Duluth Minnesotian.* Foster repeated in print his glowing predic-

*Charlemagne Tower, Jr. (right), his sister, and her husband (second from right) pose with Isaac P. Beck (left), treasurer of the family's
Duluth and Iron Range Railroad. In 1897, Tower, Jr., was named U.S. Ambassador to Austria-Hungary. The Tower family symbolizes
the faith of investors in the growing city of Duluth. Courtesy, Minnesota Historical Society*

Camille Poirier, pictured here in front of the Clark House, described his water supply system as "a large hogshead put on a cart." Water was taken from Lake Superior and used without benefit of filtration or chlorine. Courtesy, Northeast Minnesota Historical Center

tions about the region's development, yet in his first issue he cautioned would-be settlers who hoped to share in this rich future:

> Newcomers should comprehend that Duluth is at present a small place and that hotel and boarding home accommodation is extremely limited; however, lumber is cheap and shanties can be built. Everyone should bring blankets and come prepared to rough it at first.

In May 1869 Jay Cooke's principal agent, former surveyor General George B. Sargent, strode into Duluth and immediately took command of all of Cooke's business interests. Indeed, he took command of the entire community. Sargent had been hired by Cooke to oversee all of the financier's Lake Superior enterprises and to act as his personal representative. In the words of one of Sargent's fellow '69ers, "General Sargent claimed to own the world, loved a glass of wine, was liberal, advertised Duluth abroad, and he really is one of the founders of Duluth."

On lots which his old associate George Stuntz had sold him along Superior Street, Sargent oversaw construction of Duluth's first bank (commonly known as "Cooke's bank" or "Stone's bank"), where he installed George C. Stone as president. He directed construction of the community's first real hotel, the Clark House, on Superior Street between First and Second Avenues West. The hotel, which Sargent named for the proprietors of E.W. Clark and Company, one of Cooke's Philadelphia banking associates, would for the next decade be the center of high society on the Lake Superior frontier. James Egan would remember it as

> . . . a great figure in those days. All the bloods boarded there, parties were held, the ladies young and old of the city assembled, and the gentlemen in swallow-tailed coats and kids welcomed them to the lancers and the waltz . . . The banquets, the games, the rejoicing in that house cannot be told in public.

All along Superior Street, which was simply a mud and gravel thoroughfare cut along a ridge on the forested hillside, lots were being staked out, timber was being cleared, and homes and business buildings were rising. More buildings were being raised south of Superior Street from its intersection with Lake Avenue.

Then, as now, that intersection marked the very heart of Duluth. Much of the property on which this construction activity was taking place was owned by Jay Cooke's Western Land Association, under the proprietorship of George Sargent.

The company held title to nearly 7,000 parcels in and about Duluth, a fact which caused no small concern to some of the independent-minded settlers of the 1850s who correctly perceived that their community was falling into the hands of a few wealthy, absentee landlords. Yes, Duluth was Jay Cooke's town. The Philadelphian owned not only the railroad and the grain elevator, but nearly all of the city's prime commercial land.

The timber industry burgeoned to provide lumber to build the railroads and build the town. Roger S. Munger, who arrived in early 1869, established a small mill near Lake Avenue on the bayfront. He would later reminisce:

> The hills of Duluth furnished me for a long time with the finest quality of pine, and by the time I was in operation, and the rush had set in, I couldn't begin to supply the demand. I got more machinery and started another mill up the St. Louis River [on the site of the old Oneota Lumber Company] from which every day the lumber would be rafted down to Duluth . . . The hills of Duluth and out on Minnesota Point were dotted by thousands of tents, all kinds of the rudest kinds of shacks, and all those thousands were clambering for lumber in order that they might erect houses. It was a good business and I made money rapidly.

In the winter of 1869-1870 one of Munger's largest lumber customers was the Union Improvement and Elevator Company, yet another Jay Cooke enterprise. The company was building a 350,000-bushel capacity grain terminal, equipped with the most modern steam apparatus, on the lakeshore near Sidney Luce's warehouse. Union Improvement and the Lake Superior and Mississippi Railroad also began work on extensive docks to bring trains to Elevator A and on a stone and timber breakwater to shelter the vessels which would call there from the fury of Lake Superior.

In November 1869 the first telegraph link between the Head of the Lakes and the rest of the world was established. On November 12 the city fathers of St. Paul wired the Duluth office of the

Northwestern Telegraph Company: "To Duluth City—St. Paul City, head of the Great River, sends greetings to Duluth, sister of the Lakes and Gateway of the Seas." The citizens of the Zenith City immediately responded: "To St. Paul City—The Great Lakes answers the Great River; the electric tie in words is well; the iron tie in deeds is better. The metropolis of Minnesota hails the Capital." Duluth was overcoming its isolation.

In the winter of 1869-1870 the shipping industry, which would play a major role in the evolving history of both Duluth and Superior, was spurred by the construction of the largest vessel yet built at the Head of the Lakes. The *Chaska*, a 72-foot, 49-ton schooner, was built by Lewis H. Merritt, his son, Alfred, and Henry S. Ely of Oneota. With Alfred Merritt as captain, the *Chaska* engaged in the maritime commerce of western Lake Superior for little more than a year when, during a riotous storm in August 1871, the wooden craft was tossed upon a beach near Ontonagan, Michigan, and battered to matchwood. The crew managed to escape with their lives and the enterprising Merritts later procured another schooner, the *Handy*, which fared better.

While Duluth established itself as a Great Lakes shipping center, it also became an important link in the rapidly expanding railroad industry. In early 1870 Jay Cooke and Company became the financial agent for the Northern Pacific Railroad, a line which would eventually span the continent. The road was granted a half interest in that portion of the Lake Superior and the Mississippi which ran from Duluth to Thompson Junction near the present community of Carlton. Here the first track on the Northern Pacific's westward march was laid on February 15, 1870.

In addition to laying plans to capture the grain traffic from western Minnesota and the then unplowed expanses of the northern Great Plains, the Northern Pacific also hoped to tap Minnesota's iron stores. The railroad's directors appropriated half a million dollars to erect charcoal furnaces and rolling mills in or near Duluth to produce rails. Jay Cooke and Company advertised: "There are mountains of iron ore within the [railroad's] land grant, from which the road will undoubtedly, and at an early day, supply itself with rails and other iron." It appeared certain that both grain

and iron would soon pour over the docks of the lakehead; the optimism of the community's citizens and financial backers could not be restrained.

Cognizant of all this, the Minnesota Legislature on March 6, 1870, officially made Duluth a city with an aldermanic form of government. Included in the new city were the townsites of Rice's Point, Portland, Endion, Middleton, and Upper and Lower Duluth (Duluth, North Duluth, and Cowell's Addition to Duluth). On April 4 Joshua B. Culver was elected Duluth's first mayor. In his inaugural speech, Mayor Culver would declare:

> Duluth commences her existence under the most favorable and auspicious circumstances. Nature has placed her at the head of navigation upon our great chain of water communication with the Atlantic, and railroads are about to unite her with the Northwest and the Pacific Ocean. She stands, admitted by all as destined to be one of the great cities of the West.

That August the Lake Superior and Mississippi railroad was completed between St. Paul and Duluth. For most of the last 15 miles from Fond du Lac to Elevator A on the outer harbor, the line ran along wooden trestleworks and dikes built over the St. Louis River and across the swampy backwaters of St. Louis and Superior bays. By year's end there was daily train service between Duluth and St. Paul and the Northern Pacific was plodding slowly but steadily toward the western farm belt. The first cargo of grain was not, however, sent down the lakes until May 30, 1871, when the steamer *St. Paul* left Duluth with 11,500 bushels of wheat.

Citizens on both the Minnesota and Wisconsin sides of the lakehead saw the pressing need for harbor improvements and lobbied their state legislatures and the federal government for funds. As early as 1869 proposals to dig a canal through Minnesota Point were again being raised, but that year the Army Corps of Engineers decided instead to build piers at the natural harbor entry opposite Superior, and dredge channels along the seven-mile length of Superior Bay to Duluth.

Pine timber for railroads, warehouses, and residential uses made sawmilling a booming business beginning in 1870. The main mills were located on Rice's Point and along the adjacent St. Louis Bay. Logs were cut along both the North and South shores of Lake Superior as well as along the watershed of the St. Louis River and were boomed and rafted across the lake bays to the mills. By 1920, the timber industry had all but vanished from Duluth. Courtesy, Duluth Public Library

Two Merritt family boats, probably the Chaska *and the* Handy, *lay anchored in the bay. The* Chaska *was destroyed in an 1871 gale, ending a brief career. Courtesy, Northeast Minnesota Historical Center*

But Minnesota interests persisted in their demands for a man-made channel to the inner harbor—the need for such a canal was emphatically illustrated when the tempestuous Lake Superior made rubble of the breakwater on the outer harbor even before it was finished—and in March 1870 the Minnesota Legislature chartered the Minnesota Canal and Harbor Improvement Commission to dig a waterway, dredge channels and "construct and maintain such necessary piers, wharves and landings . . . as may be deemed necessary for commercial purposes." Jay Cooke's two railroads became the principal parties in this commission. A contract for the ship canal was let to W.W. Williams and Company, and that fall the firm's steam dredge *Ishpeming* began to chew its way through the sands of Minnesota Point.

Superior business interests and city officials, already snubbed in losing their bid to be the Lake Superior and Mississippi's northern railhead, saw this project as a threat to their community's economic well-being and filed suit in state and federal courts to have the dredging halted. The federal government joined with the Wisconsin plaintiffs. Legal entanglements and the harsh northern winter combined to call a stop to the project. But in the spring of 1871, with the legal questions still unresolved, Williams and Company recommenced work. On June 9 U.S. Supreme Court Justice Samuel F. Miller ordered the Minnesota defendants to "absolutely desist and abstain from digging, excavating and constructing . . . the said canal."

However, word of the judge's ruling was telegraphed to Duluth three days before a federal marshal could arrive to execute the order. During the three days, the *Ishpeming* worked round the clock moving earth to join harbor and lake. A large contingent of

citizens turned out with picks and shovels to aid the cause. By the morning of June 12 a small channel had been opened. Because the inner harbor was some six inches higher than the level of the lake, water pressure served to widen the cut and when the federal marshal arrived that afternoon he could only watch as crowds cheered the steam tug *Fero*, the first vessel to pass through the Duluth Ship Canal.

Superior howled in protest. While some citizens threatened physical action to plug the unnatural entry, the city's counsel sought further legal recourse. Duluth interests agreed to post a $100,000 bond to underwrite construction of a dam from Rice's Point to Minnesota Point to forever separate the harbors of Duluth and Superior. During 1872 the Northern Pacific erected a mile-long timber, stone, and steel dike to divide the waters of Superior Bay. But the following winter ice, wind, and water currents combined—perhaps with the help of some good citizens of both Duluth and Superior—to destroy the barrier. Since 1873 the Twin Ports of Duluth-Superior have shared, albeit jealously at times, one harbor with two entries.

The opening of the Duluth canal proved to have a beneficial effect which its promoters had not anticipated. Currents flowing through the channel carried away a considerable amount of rotting timber and mucky islets which had infested the harbor. In fact, one of Duluth's original townsites—Fremont—was thus swept out into Lake Superior and lost forever.

In 1873 Duluth was truly booming. It had a population in excess of 5,000 and hosted a wide range of civic and social organizations which signaled that city was becoming a metropolitan center. There was a regular police force and a sizeable volunteer fire department, although in June 1870 the first chief of police had absconded, never to be seen again, with a large

Railroad access to the Duluth waterfront was a necessity. It was a well-established reality by the time this photo was taken on the Superior Bay side of Rice's Point in the early 1870s. Courtesy, Northeast Minnesota Historical Center

Fire fighters, dressed in red flannel shirts, black belts, and blue trousers, gathered at the Clark House for the annual Firemen's Ball. Walter Van Brunt, Edmund Ingalls, George Spencer, and John Lavaque were among the volunteer fire fighters pictured in this 1881 photograph. Courtesy, Duluth Public Library

construction payroll, and in October 1871 the fire department's first engine had been engulfed in flames and destroyed while preparing to answer its first fire alarm. Several churches—Episcopal, Presbyterian, Methodist, Roman Catholic, Baptist, Congregational, and Lutheran—had been organized and had erected edifices.

By 1870 the Young Men's Christian Association was active, and in 1872 the Duluth Bethel Society was founded. Thomas Foster's weekly *Duluth Minnesotian* was receiving keen competition from R.C. Mitchell's *Duluth Tribune.* There were, in addition to George Sargent's banking house, at least two other financial houses in the city. Wholesale and retail businesses—ranging from grocers to jewelers, from hardware peddlers to haberdashers— flourished. And in 1873 the Duluth Iron and Steel Company, with John H. Shoenberger of Pittsburgh as president and manager, opened a blast furnace on Rice's Point.

Then, on September 18, 1873, the unthinkable happened. The financial house of Jay Cooke and Company collapsed. Even with his vast riches, Cooke had overextended himself in pressing the rapid expansion of the Northern Pacific. He simply ran out of money. Jay Cooke's failure pushed the entire nation's economy into panic, into depression. Newspaperman R.C. Mitchell would later describe the effect that failure had on the Head of the Lakes:

Of course all work on the Northern Pacific was stopped at once, and as it was not known when it would be resumed there was an utter state of demoralization, especially in Duluth which had sprung up like magic and whose business chiefly depended upon it being the supply point for the Northern Pacific Railroad. I am safe in saying that inside of 60 days more than half of the men engaged in trade in Duluth went out of business, many of them going bankrupt and the others selling out for what they could get . . . and left the place.

Duluth's population plummeted, by one account sinking to a mere 1,300. Once again the community had been catapulted from boom to bust.

The city of Duluth, like its patron Jay Cooke and like many engaged in trade there, had also overextended itself, issuing bonds and underwriting both civic and industrial improvements on nothing stronger than the promise of uninterrupted prosperity. In early 1874 city officials petitioned Congress for a quarter-million-dollar grant (later denied) and asked the Minnesota Legislature to exempt them from payment of state tax levies.

For the next three years a bitter dispute raged between political factions in the floundering city. One side, predominantly Democratic, argued vociferously for "repudiation" of Duluth's obligations, a process which had been used by the former states of the Confederacy to wipe out their mammoth Civil War debts. The opposing parties, championed by Dr. Vespasion Smith who had been elected mayor in April 1873 and re-elected in 1874, fought to retain Duluth's status as a city and somehow reduce and retire its bonded debt.

In late 1876 a compromise was struck by Mayor John Drew and the Minnesota Legislature whereby Duluth's city charter was simply allowed to expire. A village form of government was to be established, according to the Minnesota statutes of 1876, in "the settled part of Duluth . . . under a promise to pay off its [the city's] indebtedness at 50 cents on the dollar through the judge of the District Court." On March 12, 1877, the Duluth City Council met for the last time, turned an empty safe and its fire-fighting equipment over to the village and officially disbanded. The new village was limited to that area between the ship canal, Mesaba Avenue, Third Street, and Third Avenue East and could not be expanded until Judge O.P. Stearns endorsed the retirement of certain amounts of the old city's debts. The process would require the better part of the next decade.

Schiller-Hubbard Company, located at 404 West Superior Street, was the leading wholesale and retail cigar store in 1890s Duluth. It began at 26 West Superior Street in about 1880. Courtesy, Northeast Minnesota Historical Center

However, commercial activity in Duluth rebounded from Jay Cooke's collapse much faster than municipal finances. The crash of 1873 had driven people throughout the nation to search for new livelihoods and new methods of staying alive. Many became the sodbusters of the Great Plains, the produce of whose farms would, as had been prophesied, flow eastward over the docks of Duluth. In 1880 the Lake Superior Elevator Company, working with the then-reviving Northern Pacific Railroad, built a terminal with a one million-bushel capacity near the base of Rice's Point. Other gargantuan grain storehouses would soon rise on the Duluth and Superior waterfronts so that by 1886 the Twin Ports harbor boasted a combined capacity in excess of 22 million bushels.

In 1881 the Duluth Board of Trade was organized to better cope with the growing influx of wheat to the port's elevators. That year the city's grain receipts were listed at 3,332,176 bushels; that figure would skyrocket to 22,425,730 bushels just five years later. In that time the board's membership also climbed from a dozen to more than 200.

On November 27, 1886, Duluth's grain trade was dealt a serious setback when Elevator A, the port's pioneer terminal, and the adjacent Elevator Q were destroyed by fire. The blaze killed at least two men, consumed nearly half a million bushels of wheat, corn, flax, and oats valued at $275,000, and according to one report, "The Chicago grain market took a sudden upswing upon learning of the Duluth elevator losses."

Beginning in 1880 there was a renewed flurry of railroad speculation. Several lines laid plans for Duluth or Superior railheads in order to be able to compete with the Northern Pacific and the St. Paul and Duluth. The latter road was the successor to the Lake Superior and Mississippi which, with the downfall of Jay Cooke, also fell upon hard times (though it was reorganized in 1876).

During the summer of 1881 Duluth was abuzz with the hope that the Duluth and Winnipeg Railroad, then carving a grade for itself along the town's steep western hillside, would soon link with the Canadian Pacific Railroad which was then forging a steel trail across Canada. Although this link would have been more economical for the Canadian line, Canadians were opposed to routing their railroad through the United States, and chose to build north of Lake Superior. Duluth's hopes were never realized.

In the early 1880s a syndicate of Eastern capitalists headed by Charlemagne Tower had determined to develop the Lake Vermilion iron fields, which had been discovered in the 1860s. Duluth became the headquarters for this development and home to both the Minnesota Iron Company and the Duluth and Iron Range Railway. Men and machinery marched north along the Vermilion Trail laid out by George Stuntz nearly two decades earlier to accommodate the ill-fated Vermilion gold rush. Mineral speculation again became an avocation, if not a vocation, for a sizeable number of Duluthians. Yet Duluth lost the distinction of being the shipping center for the Vermilion ore when Tower built his railroad to Agate Bay, some 25 miles down the North Shore. There he also erected massive wooden docks from which the iron could be loaded by gravity directly from rail cars to the holds of waiting vessels for shipment to lower lakes steel mills.

On July 3, 1884, amid great pomp and circumstance at the wilderness iron mine in the frontier town of Tower which bore its financial patron's name, the first Minnesota ore was loaded aboard wooden rail cars for the 68-mile trip to Agate Bay. Charlemagne Tower, Jr., who served as railroad president and monitored his father's investments from his offices in Duluth, rode the rails that day with a delegation of civic and business leaders from Duluth and from eastern financial houses.

When the train reached the new port community (soon to be named Two Harbors) and the ore was dumped into the waiting steamer Hecla, Tower wired his father in Philadelphia: "All well contented with our day." It can only be surmised that the elder Tower, who never did visit his Lake Superior iron operations, was also well contented; he had spent an estimated $1.75 million of his own money to make possible this opening of Minnesota's iron age.

The grain and mineral renaissance also spawned a revival of Duluth's timber industry. Several small sawmills had been opened in the early 1870s, but many of them failed along with Jay Cooke. By the early 1880s a new wave of mills had risen, several locating on Rice's Point while others stretched out along the St. Louis Bay and river as far as Oneota. White pine was the mainstay of nearly all, and that pine was harvested from the forests in and around Duluth. It was often transported to the mills down the rivers and across the bays of the lakehead on rafts. By the mid-1880s these sawmills were cutting 10 million board feet of timber a year.

Harbor improvements couldn't keep pace with this rapid industrial advancement. By 1886 the Army Engineers had located an office and a boat yard in Duluth; and the following year the city officially surrendered title to the ship canal to the federal government, as city fathers preferred that the federal government pay for the canal's improvements and upkeep. The Army Engineers had earlier built piers a quarter mile into Lake Superior at the canal entry and erected a lighthouse on the southern pierhead. The editors of the *Duluth Daily News* would boast in 1888:

> The whole harbor system affords a perfect refuge against storms and abundant room for the mercantile marine of the entire chain of lakes. Duluth harbor proper is easily and safely entered from the lake through a ship canal nearly 300 feet wide and 1,500 feet long, running nearly parallel with the North Shore. The canal is perfectly straight in line with the track of vessels coming up the lakes, and had a depth of nearly 25 feet which is steadily maintained by the ebb and flow of the current between the lake and the harbor.

Yet that current was a continual plague to shipmasters who at times had to fight to keep their vessels from being turned broadside in the channel. In the inner harbor shallow dockside drafts and shifting sandbars also troubled vesselmen. Yet by 1888, 2,200 ships carrying an aggregate cargo of 1,943,236 tons would visit the harbor in a single season.

Above: Fur trader Peter J. Peterson's solidly built frame house, Duluth's oldest surviving residence, went up in Fond du Lac in 1867. Its foundation came from the nearby Mission Creek Quarry. By the 1880s, Fond du Lac was a quiet rural area with transportation to downtown Duluth by train. Courtesy, Minnesota Historical Society

Below: According to the 1870 census of Duluth, the city had 3,131 residents, the majority of whom were foreign-born. The immigrants included 33.5 percent Swedish, 14.5 percent Irish, 13.8 percent German, 13.1 percent Canadian, and 13 percent Norwegian. Sixty percent of the foreign-born male labor force were common laborers, and 15.1 percent were carpenters. Courtesy, Library of Congress

Yes, Duluth was booming again. When Minnesota conducted its state census in 1885 the community's population was listed at 18,036. That compared to 3,470 in the federal census five years earlier. By 1888 there were an estimated 33,000-plus residents.

Residential neighborhoods spread east and west. Many of the first wave of the rising upper and middle business classes built strikingly ornate yet sturdy family homes along the streets and avenues immediately north and east of the heart of the city. The Duluth Street Railway Company, organized in 1881, inaugurated service in the spring of 1883 with mule-drawn cars carrying passengers for a nickel fare.

By 1887 streetcar tracks ran from 23rd Avenue West to 22nd Avenue East. Citizens of more distant suburbs could ride commuter trains of the St. Paul and Duluth or the Duluth and Iron Range which had run a line from Two Harbors to Duluth in 1885. By the late 1880s the Lakeside Land Company was developing family housing projects in New London and Lester Park. The firm also built a large resort hotel on the Lester River which the *Duluth Daily News* of 1888 predicted would be

*Mule-drawn streetcar ser-
vice began on a continuous
basis in 1883, with a fare
of five cents. Passengers
could travel from Eighth
Avenue West to Third
Avenue East on Superior
Street or from Eighth
Avenue West to Rice's
Point. Courtesy, Duluth
Public Library*

*Elevator A and the break-
water are barely visible on
the waterfront in this view
from Mesaba Avenue in
1887. At this time,
25 percent of the ships
arriving were still powered
by wind, and steel ships
were just making their
appearance. Courtesy,
Duluth Public Library*

. . . a model of its kind, affording all the comforts and pleasures and less of the discomforts of the eastern summer resorts. Here the "hay fever brigade" may find the balm of Gilead, a surcease from sorrow and pain, for no aching head, no aching lungs, no aching heart can long resist the magnetism of the glorious scenes of the bracing air that Duluth offers to all.

Another hay fever haven of the day was Minnesota Point, where the village of Park Point had been incorporated following the failure of Duluth as a city. The Minnesota Point Street Railway Company carried tourists and residents alike from the south side of the ship canal to resorts and encampments where, according to the *Duluth Daily News* "the breezes are never at rest, where the waves are seldom still, and cut off from the busy world by the waters of the great unsalted sea, one may rest in peace."

To the west the city of West Duluth, which its founders claimed would be "the new Pittsburgh," was established in 1888. Its citizens were to be the managers and the work force of the Duluth Iron and Steel company, then building a blast furnace and rolling mill near the banks of the St. Louis River, and the Minnesota Car Works Company, at the same time erecting a vast industrial complex to manufacture railroad rolling stock. West Duluth soon engulfed all of the townsite of Oneota.

As the population multiplied so did the Zenith City's need for educational facilities. By 1886 Duluth's public schools system, under Superintendent Robert E. Denfield, who would mastermind educational affairs for more than three decades, had an enrollment of 1,600 pupils in eight locations, including the new high school at First Avenue East and Third Street. There were also by the late 1880s four parochial schools, among them the forerunner of Duluth Cathedral, which had been opened by the Sisters of St. Benedict in 1881.

St. Luke's Hospital was founded in an old blacksmith shop by the Episcopal Reverend J.A. Cummings in 1882, in response to a typhoid epidemic ravaging the Twin Ports; Cummings would recall:

Three or four chairs and three beds with bedding was all I could gather at the time, and a stove donated by the British government from the emigrant station. No sooner had the furniture been installed than an old man, a charity case, sought care at the hospital . . . I placed an advertisement in the papers that the hospital was open, and in one week we had 12 patients. At the end of the month there were 29 being cared for in the little shack.

In 1888 the Sisters of St. Benedict established St. Mary's Hospital in Duluth's West End when another typhoid epidemic erupted.

Throughout the 1880s, as the Lake Superior country once again boomed, the village of Duluth continued to pay off the debts of the defunct city and expand its boundaries. By early 1887 the village retired the last of the old bonds, and the Minnesota Legislature again sanctioned incorporation of the city of Duluth. On March 15, 1887, John B. Sutphin, who had served as village president, was elected mayor. Among the first public impovements endorsed by the new city fathers was the laying of cedar black pavement along Superior Street which had, according to one observer, become "something terrible" with horses being "mired right in the business section of the city."

In 1888 the city council created four city parks; 49 acres for Cascade Park atop the bluff immediately north of the business section; 69 acres for Chester Park on the east hillside; one city block at 10th Avenue East and Third Street for Portland Square; and according to the city ordinance of the day, the area known as Lincoln Bank "following the bank of Miller's Creek at the West End." Among other social features was the Grand Opera House, built at the corner of Fourth Avenue West and Superior Street in 1883 by Roger Munger, who had been a kingpin of commercial, civic and social affairs since his arrival in 1869. In addition to hosting some of the best dramatic troupes and theatrical performers of the day the Opera House also provided a first home for the Kitchi Gammi Club, described in 1888 by the *Daily News* as Duluth's "principal social club . . . its annual reception is always an event of the season."

In light of all that had been accomplished, and all that seemed imminent, the editors of the *Duluth Daily News* did not consider themselves forward in proclaiming as 1888 drew to a close:

> With such possibilities of geographical position, agricultural, timber, and mineral products, and with the steadily rising wave of population composed of hardy, resolute and enterprising men sweeping over the hills and plains of the Northwest, delving in its mines, leveling its forests, cultivating its now waste places, and opening a track for the iron horse across the vast areas, what mind can conceive, or who can estimate the prodigies of growth that must come to the cities along this wonderful "pathway of empire," and especially to that one which holds the key to the entire situation at the head of the Great Lakes?

Seven streams rise behind the city and find their way to Lake Superior or the St. Louis Bay. Six form the centers of six Duluth parks: Cascade, Chester, Congdon, Lester, Lincoln, and Fairmont. Courtesy, Duluth Public Library

In 1888 the city established a park system, laying out Cascade Park and others. Many private citizens helped to build Cascade Park's elaborate masonry. Courtesy, Duluth Public Library

In 1882 the Episcopalians opened St. Luke's Hospital in an old blacksmith shop in response to the severe typhoid problem caused by water intake pipes improperly positioned in the lake. A new 38-bed facility replaced St. Luke's in 1884, and the present hospital at 10th Avenue East and First Street was completed in 1902. Courtesy, Duluth Public Library

A favorite carriage ride for Duluthians was Terrace Drive, known also as Boulevard Drive, a driveway along the face of the hill that became Duluth's famed Skyline Drive. Horses and carriages sold by Duluth Carriage Works soon gave way to automobiles, which were introduced to Duluth in 1901. Courtesy, Duluth Public Library

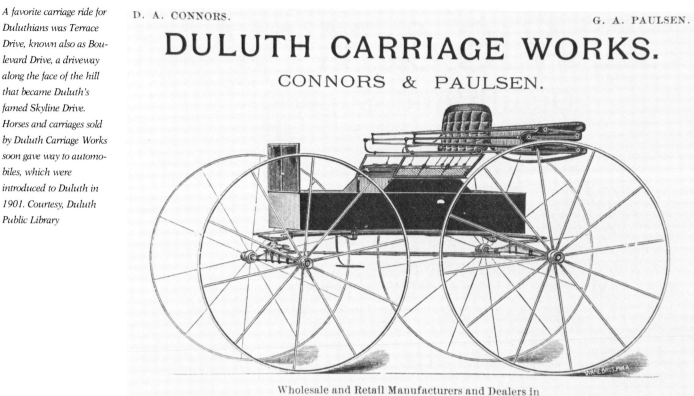

D. A. CONNORS.   G. A. PAULSEN.

DULUTH CARRIAGE WORKS.

CONNORS & PAULSEN.

Wholesale and Retail Manufacturers and Dealers in

CARRIAGES, BUGGIES, LIGHT SPRING WAGONS, SLEIGHS, CARTS, ETC.

315 West First St.   Send for Catalogue and Prices.   DULUTH, MINN.

Built in 1883 at Fourth Avenue West and Superior Street, the Grand Opera House opened with a production of Martha. *Financed by Clinton Markell and Roger Munger, Duluth's most elegant building boasted towers, oriels, panels, and narrow, arched windows. Fire destroyed the building in 1889. Courtesy, Duluth Public Library*

Courtesy, Kentucky Historical Society

J. Proctor Knott

Proctor Knott made a national laughingstock out of Duluth. Yet on his only visit to what he jokingly called "the paragon of cities," he was accorded a hero's welcome.

The Honorable J. Proctor Knott was representing the state of Kentucky in the U.S. House of Representatives when he was lobbied by some of his state's wealthy businessmen to lend his persuasive voice to a campaign to win a massive federal land grant for construction of a rail line from the St. Croix River to the Lake Superior ports of Superior and Bayfield, Wisconsin. Knott harbored serious reservations about the wisdom of such land giveaways, but he bowed to political pressures and agreed to speak on the question. On January 27, 1871, with only minutes remaining before a legislatively-imposed deadline for action on the Bayfield and St. Croix Railroad grant, Knott took the floor in the U.S. House and launched into the kind of oratory for which he was so well respected. It was apparent to all that he had done his homework, although somewhere in the process he had mistakenly identified Duluth as the northern terminus of the proposed road. His resonant tone brought all of his colleagues to attention; indeed it brought many of them to their feet as he declared:

'Duluth!' The word fell upon my ear with peculiar and indescribable charm, like the gentle murmur of a low fountain, stealing forth in the midst of roses, or the soft, sweet accents of an angel's whisper in the bright, joyous dream of sleeping innocence. Duluth!

The congressman conceded that he had never actually visited the Head of the Lakes, but he vouched for his sources of information as "gentlemen who have been so reckless of their personal safety as to venture away in those awful regions where Duluth is supposed to be." He bemoaned the calamity that "the enlightened nations of the ancient world" had never even known of Duluth's existence. His eloquent prose drew applause and laughter as he continued

. . . the fabled Atlantis, never seen save by the hallowed

vision of poesy, was in fact but another name for Duluth; the golden orchard of Hesperides was but a synonym for the beer gardens in the vicinity of Duluth. I know that if the immortal spirit of Homer could look down from another heaven . . . he would weep bitter tears that . . . it had not been his more blessed lot to crystalize in deathless song the rising glory of Duluth.

The land grant backers became edgy as Knott's wordy portrait stretched into a mural. But there was no denying the Kentuckian's rhetoric as he told how the city was "so exactly in the center of the visible universe that the skies come down precisely at the same distance all around it." He extolled the climate of the region, maintaining that:

Duluth is situated just exactly half way between the latitudes of Paris and Venice, so that the gentlemen who have inhaled the exhilirating air of the one or basked in the golden sunshine of the other must see at once that Duluth must be a place of untold delights, a terrestrial paradise fanned by the balmy zephyrs of an eternal spring, clothed with the gorgeous sheen of ever-blooming flowers, and vocal with the choicest melodies of nature's choicest songsters.

But on that chiming note the House clock chimed the end of time for action on the land grant, and Knott's true purpose was divined. Amid resounding laughter and applause, he concluded

. . . these lands which I am asked to give away, alas, are not mine to bestow. My relation to them is simply that of a trustee to an express trust. And shall I ever betray that trust? Never, sir! Rather perish Duluth! Perish the paragon of cities. Rather let the freezing cyclones of the bleak Northwest bury it forever beneath the eddying sands of the St. Croix!

Knott's jocular damnation of Duluth doomed the Bayfield and St. Croix Railroad. But his loquacious humor was so popularly received that his speech was printed and reprinted in newspapers and magazines throughout the United States. Duluth became the butt of one of the best-known jokes of the day.

But Duluth's city fathers didn't seem to mind. Rather, they reveled in the national spotlight Knott had focused on their community. In August 1890, on his only visit ever to Duluth, J. Proctor Knott was accorded a hero's reception. On August 14 he told a banquet tendered in his honor by the citizens of Duluth

Possibly the mention of the name "Duluth" may bring my own to the recollection of millions long after I shall have mouldered into dust, and everything else pertaining to my existence faded from the memory of men.

And the name of the Kentucky gentleman who killed one Lake Superior railroad is memorialized to this day by another rail line. The service center for the Duluth, Missabe & Iron Range Railway is a bustling community just north of Duluth which was originally called Proctorknott and is now known simply as Proctor.

Chapter Four

1889-1915

THE EPITOME OF PROSPERITY

The booming echoes of industrial prosperity rang across the waters of western Lake Superior and resounded from the hillsides of the Zenith City. Duluth's hardy, resolute, and enterprising citizens were forging new industry and making new fortunes on at least half a dozen fronts in the final years of the 1880s.

Railroads were drawn to Duluth and Superior like lightning to an iron rod. By the end of 1888, 10 railroads with more than 16,000 miles of track had gained entry to the wharves and warehouses of the Twin Ports. Included among these was the St. Paul, Minneapolis and Manitoba of "Empire Builder," James J. Hill. The line would eventually become the base of the continent-spanning Great Northern. Hill wedded the Manitoba to the Northern Steamship line and thus controlled a sizeable portion of the flow of commerce between the western Great Plains and the eastern Great Lakes.

Because Duluth's steep gabbro hills have their feet planted nearly in the waters of the lake, river, and bays which constitute the city's eastern face, the railways competed bitterly to command the narrow strip of level land along that face. City fathers, fearful that this competition would turn potential business away from Duluth, organized the Duluth Terminal Railway. The company was to provide access at equitable rates to the city's commercial and industrial districts to all who wished to use it. In early 1889, the *Duluth Daily News* described the grand plan envisioned by the city officials and civic leaders:

Banker and financier J. Pierpont Morgan formed J.P. Morgan and Company in 1875. The company financed government, reorganized railroads, and formed the U.S. Steel Corporation in 1901. The model city created in 1913 around the Duluth steel plant became known as Morgan Park in 1914 to honor Morgan, who had died in 1913. Courtesy, Library of Congress

Paul B. Gaylord,

PHOTOGRAPHER.

A Large Assortment of

STEREOSCOPIC VIEWS

Of the Famous Lake Superior Scenery, to which additions are being constantly made.

GERMAN AMERICAN BLOCK,
West Superior,

DULUTH, MINN.

Photographer Paul Gaylord, an early settler, was responsible for most views of Duluth made in the 1880s. Scenic attractions of the city often decorated early advertisements. Courtesy, Duluth Public Library

Railroad Street, the warehouse district, and several ships in the harbor are visible in this 1880s view down Third Avenue West. Ray T. Lewis, Duluth's mayor from 1894 to 1896, reportedly occupied the three-story brick building at right center. Courtesy, Duluth Public Library

Beginning at the corner of Sixth Avenue West and Railroad [Street] alley the line runs westward to the end of Grassy Point, a distance of about six miles, at which place a bridge shall be built at some future time. At 14th Avenue West begins another line which extends the whole length of Rice's Point to the Northern Pacific bridge, thence crossing by a bridge over the harbor to Minnesota Point and along its nearly seven miles of length, from the canal, which will also be bridged, to the natural entry.

From downtown and across much of Rice's Point the terminal railway would run along an elevated trestlework so as not to disrupt existing trackage and to eventually allow two tiers of rail traffic to flow into and out of Duluth at the same time. Part, but not all, of the trestlework was erected, and the terminal railway was a success although it never entirely lived up to expectations.

Among the first enterprises to take advantage of this rail activity was the Duluth Imperial Mill. The milling company, organized in 1888 by a group of Duluthians headed by Roger S. Munger, was located near the foot of Sixth Avenue West and represented the first large-scale attempt to deflect some of the grain pouring through the Twin Ports and manufacture it into flour. By the end of 1889 the Imperial had the capacity to mill 8,000 barrels of flour a day. Also in 1889, the Minnesota Car Company (producer of rail cars) and the Duluth Iron and Steel Company began production in West Duluth.

At the same time the federal government was undertaking a major improvement project 450 miles east of Duluth which would have an immeasurable impact on the Head of the Lakes. Uncle Sam was spending $7 million to widen the channels and enlarge the locks at Sault Ste. Marie. A new lock would measure 800 feet by 100 feet with a 21-foot draft. In the words of one observer, "With the completion of these works . . . the capacity of vessels navigating Lake Superior will be greatly increased, and its commerce will be augmented with the development of the country beyond all present power of computation."

Alexander McDougall was intent upon capitalizing on this new maritime development. The Scottish-born lakes captain and marine entrepreneur had by himself financed, constructed, and launched his first steel barge on the Duluth waterfront in 1888. His

Left: *The whaleback SS* Thomas Wilson *and a consort barge rest at Duluth dock in about 1900. After colliding with the wooden coal carrier George G. Hadley, the* Thomas Wilson *went down in two minutes, taking nine men to their deaths June 7, 1902. The* Hadley *was salvaged later, but the* Thomas Wilson *still lies on the bottom of the lake off Eighth Avenue East. Courtesy, Canal Park Visitors Center*

Alexander McDougall

Captain Alexander McDougall's dream boat actually had the look of a nightmare—it looked like no vessel ever before envisioned. But it cost less to construct and carried more cargo than anything afloat, and it could cut through the heaviest seas the Great Lakes could spawn. McDougall's dream boat would revolutionize maritime commerce.

Alexander McDougall was born on the Isle of Islay, Scotland, on March 16, 1845. He emigrated with his family to Canada in 1854, settling in Collingwood, Ontario, on Lake Huron's Georgian Bay. At age 16 McDougall began his career as a sailor, shipping out as a deckhand on what seemed like an endless stream of lakes steamers and sailing craft. By 1870 he had climbed those ships' ladders to earn his master's license and received his first command from Captain Thomas Wilson of the Anchor Line.

For the next two decades McDougall sailed the lakes for Wilson, worked as a commercial fisherman on Lake Superior and ran a stevedoring operation from his adopted home of Duluth. While piloting one of Wilson's wooden monsters through the lakes' narrow and treacherous channels he dreamed of building a cheaper and safer steel ship. He would later recall that he laid plans for a boat

> . . . with a flat bottom designed to carry the greatest cargo on the least water, with rounded top so that water could not stay on board; with a spoon-shaped bow to best follow the line of the strain with the least use of the rudder, and with turrets on deck for passage into the interior of the hull.

McDougall proudly named his vessell a "whaleback," for its low-slung, water-shedding profile. Veteran lakesmen, to whom he appealed for financial support to build such ships, scoffed at his design and called it a "pig boat" because of its blunt, hog-like snout. So McDougall, confident in the worth of his dream boat, decided to build it himself. Using his stevedores as shipwrights he constructed the first whaleback, a barge measuring 191 feet by 22 feet, at a yard he owned on the Duluth waterfront. Emmeline Ross McDougall apparently didn't share her husband's confidence, for as the barge slid into Superior Bay on a balmy June day in 1888

she was heard confiding to a friend, "There goes our last dollar."

But the whaleback proved an immediate success. McDougall won financial backing from Colgate Hoyt, an associate of John D. Rockefeller, and the American Steel Barge Company was incorporated. The firm soon moved its yard to more spacious quarters in West Superior, Wisconsin. In the next decade, more than 40 whalebacks—barges and steamers—were launched for the Great Lakes bulk trade. Most saw many years of profitable service.

In 1893 McDougall launched his most famous whaleback, the *Christopher Columbus*. He built it for the tourist trade at the 1894 Chicago World's Fair. The *Columbus* had four decks, posh Victorian salons with etched plate windows and skylights, leather furnishings and marble trim, and could carry 7,500 passengers from downtown Chicago to neighboring Jackson Park. He would describe the *Columbus* as "probably the most wonderful ship contracted for and constructed up to that time."

McDougall also had other visions for his dream boat. He designed a huge passenger/mail carrier for transatlantic runs and a whaleback man-o'-war. But neither craft was ever built save as a model, which the designer tested in special flotation tanks he had built into his Duluth home.

Unfortunately, the whaleback's simple yet sturdy design had limitations which would eventually lead to its abandonment. McDougall could not build a ship with a beam greater than 45 feet without inserting structural supports throughout the hull, thus reducing cargo space and complicating loading and unloading. Other steel vessels were soon being built which were far larger and carried far greater tonnages than the whalebacks. Yet all had been inspired by McDougall's radical design. The last whaleback the pioneer shipbuilder built—a ship he named for himself—reflected the design changes which were making his dream boat obsolete. The steamer *Alexander McDougall* was launched in Superior in 1898 and measured 413 feet by 50 feet. It had the traditional whale's stern and midsection, but its snout was replaced with the bevelled bow now common to lakes carriers.

Alexander McDougall died in 1923, aware that his dream boat was still regarded by many mariners as a laughable nightmare. He was also well aware that his dream had helped transform the face of Great Lakes commerce.

Grain tycoon George Spencer's residence, an example of Oliver Traphagen's residential work, is shown as it looked in 1892 (below), and 90 years later, after it had been divided into apartments (right). Courtesy, Duluth Public Library

revolutionary whaleback design was described by one lakes-watcher as "peculiar and rather demoralizing to one's ideas of 'stately ships that ride the seas.'"

But McDougall's whalebacks proved highly efficient in carrying Minnesota iron down the Great Lakes, and in 1889 he won the backing of several of John D. Rockefeller's lieutenants and formed the American Steel Barge Company. Some of Duluth's downtown business interests opposed the noise potential of a major shipbuilding operation, and McDougall moved his enterprise to West Superior where, in a friendlier setting, he built a substantial fleet of barges and steamers.

Duluth's religious, social, and civic institutions paralleled the city's industrial expansion. In 1889 the Roman Catholic Diocese of Duluth was created and the Most Reverend James Golrick was appointed the first bishop of Duluth. The diocesan chancery was located in the old Cathedral of the Sacred Heart, built in 1870 and razed by fire in 1892.

City government acquired a new home in 1889 when a city hall, which Mayor Sutphin declared would be large enough to meet Duluth's needs "for several generations to come," and a brownstone police station and jail were built along Superior Street near Second Avenue East. Both buildings are still standing.

That summer the police department was faced with its most trying enforcement task to date. Laborers working on municipal sewer projects walked off the job, demanding higher wages. Only one private contractor agreed to the pay demands. But workers who had not received raises insisted that those who had received them continue to take part in their strike. A fracas ensued and the police had to be called to prevent violence between the two labor factions. However, according to one man who had witnessed the incident:

On the following day, July 6, 1889, the strikers, reinforced by a crowd of ruffians from the city and Superior, armed with guns and revolvers and rocks, came again to where the men were at work. And again the police were called, but this time they met the opposition that resulted in the riot. Every officer of the force took part in the riot, and every officer was either shot or sustained bruises during the fight. The strikers were overpowered after a short time, and the trouble came to an end.

The strike was broken and, according to one report, four of the rioters died from wounds received in their own violent protest. The citizens of Duluth took up a subscription and presented each of the 28 members of the police force with a gold medallion for valor during the riot.

Another source of trouble for the police in 1889 was Wilhelm Boeing, who arrived in the city from Detroit late that autumn and claimed title to the property on either side of the Duluth Ship Canal. His claim was apparently based on a questionable fractional interest in several lots. He advertised in the local papers that, unless the city of Duluth paid him $100,000 for land which had been taken from him for construction of the canal, he would halt all vessels from crossing his property.

Boeing strung a heavy rope across the channel entry, only to have it cut three times—once by police and twice by passing ships. Police stepped in again when Boeing attempted to stretch an iron chain across the harbor entry. They arrested him and offered him the option of facing civil and criminal charges for obstructing traffic and destroying property or leaving town immediately. Boeing was never heard from in Duluth again.

The city was not so easily rid of another commercial gadfly of the 1880s and 1890s. He was Frederick B. Prentice, a native of Toledo, Ohio, who had been a trader at Ashland, Wisconsin, when the Treaty of La Pointe was signed in 1854. Two years later he paid $8,000 for an undivided half-interest in a square mile of property at the Head of the Lakes which the treaty had deeded to the Ojibway Chief Buffalo. Prentice would not assert his claim to what became known as the "Buffalo claim" until the mid-1880s, by which time the tract had been divided and subdivided into some 2,600 parcels which constituted the heart of Duluth's business district.

Over a several-year period Prentice filed a score of lawsuits in federal court in St. Paul against one or more of the property owners, seeking either the return of his land or payment for it based on current values. And that current value was worth millions. (William Spalding, whose namesake hotel was opened on the corner of Fifth Avenue West and Superior Street in 1889, would claim that single structure had "raised and maintained the values for several blocks in its vicinity from 100 to 500 percent.") Spalding was only one of those against whom Prentice sought judgment. He also sued the Northern Pacific and its Western Land Association, the single largest property owners in the old Buffalo tract.

Yet each time Prentice hailed Duluthians into court he failed to appear and lost his suit by default. But the mere threat of litigation hung like a pall over Duluth's business community and served to drive away potential investors and industries. In 1890, one Duluth business countersued the former trader and won a court order restraining further legal action on his part. Prentice appealed that ruling, but it was upheld. Frederick Prentice was vanquished without ever having won a single court battle against any of his Duluth adversaries. However, it has long been rumored that he nevertheless reaped great gain from his unsuccessful attempts to monopolize the Zenith City of the Unsalted Seas by taking large cash settlements from numerous defendants before they ever entered a courtroom.

With the curse of Prentice removed, Duluth bustled with roisterous prosperity. Perhaps typifying this activity was the New Duluth Land Company, organized in early 1890. The firm held a large tract along the St. Louis River near Spirit Lake and, according to Charles E. Lovett, a principal in the company, "With more than 2,000 acres of fine land, admirably adapted to townsite purposes, with five miles of waterfront and good railroad advantages, everyone considered that the situation was ideal." Lovett and his partners had secured promises that several industries would locate at or near their townsite—a sawmill and furniture factory, a refrigerator plant, and an iron and brass works—and he would recall:

We held the opening sale of lots on October 28, 1890 . . . This was the most remarkable sale ever held in the Northwest. The large office of the company was filled to

W.W. Spalding's hotel was designed by architect James J. Egan of Chicago, a nationally-known hotel architect. The hotel, built on the site of Spalding's store, featured a fourth-floor dining room with a spectacular view of Lake Superior. Courtesy, Northeast Minnesota Historical Center

The Ordean Building, built in 1973-1974 as the headquarters of the Ordean Foundation and other nonprofit organizations, stands on the former Spalding Hotel site. Albert Ordean, whose estate is the source of the Ordean Foundation, came to Duluth in 1882. He was a banker and partner in Stone-Ordean-Wells, a wholesale grocery house. Photo by Jeff Frey

Duluth developed rapidly between 1880 and 1893. Ads such as this one promised solid investments in the growing city. Thousands were employed in the building of homes, flour mills, ore docks, warehouses, and lumber mills, as Duluth became the distribution point for the Mesabi and Vermilion iron ranges. Immigrants moved to Duluth in great numbers, and the city's population grew from 13,000 in 1883 to 30,000 in 1889. Courtesy, Duluth Public Library

Designed and constructed by engineer Samuel Diescher of Pittsburgh, Duluth's incline railway served the city and fascinated tourists from 1891 until 1939, when it was torn down and sold for scrap. The tracks rose from Superior Street at Seventh Avenue West to Skyline Drive, and the ride cost a nickel. Courtesy, Duluth Public Library

suffocation the evening before the doors were to be opened. With hundreds of men crowded into one room, as thick as they could stand, the room became warm and the air so foul that men fainted, and when anyone collapsed he was taken out over the heads of the crowd, as that was the only way of getting him out. One man died as a result of the experience . . . The sales amounted to $412,000.

Competing with the New Duluth Land Company was the Highland Improvement Company, a consortium of wealthy Duluthians who planned to construct and sell modest yet modern homes to the city's fast-growing middle class in a residential development (Duluth Heights) atop the rocky outcroppings which shielded the downtown business district. Highland Improvement contracted with the owners of the Duluth Street Railway Company to build an elevated tramway along Seventh Avenue West from Superior Street to the crest of the hill near Eighth Street.

The incline, as it was to be known to all in Duluth and many throughout the nation, was a mammoth iron trestlework with two sets of rails and a pair of sheet steel cars, each weighing 25,000 pounds, which were guided along the tracks by steel cable joined to the system's power source, a steam engine at the incline's hilltop terminus. When service was initiated on the incline on December 1, 1891, the *Duluth Tribune* hailed, "the dawn of a new era . . . a stupendous project which will put the Zenith City upon a metropolitan basis."

The incline gained more attention and more importance less than a year later when an ornate wooden pavilion measuring 100-by-300 feet was constructed near the tramway's upper station. Known simply as the Pavilion, it was to be Duluth's cultural and entertainment center and housed dining and dancing halls plus a 1,600-seat auditorium. On July 4, 1892, some 16,000 Duluthians attended a gala grand-opening picnic. During the next decade the Pavilion was to play host to a wide range of public and private affairs, touring theatrical and vaudeville companies, and musical concerts. A civic orchestra made its debut there in 1895 under the baton of Professor Otto Muhlbaur.

Another major entertainment center was constructed at the corner of Fifth Avenue West and Superior Street, opposite the Spalding Hotel. The Lyceum Theater was indeed an elegant structure, with seating for 1,500. Following its premiere performance on August 3, 1891, the *Tribune* predicted the Lyceum's stage would "in time be the source of much amusement. Likewise of instruction." And the newspaper gushed:

The scene in the auditorium is an enchanting one. The design, as it comes out under the shaded lights of hundreds of incandescents, is chaste and artistic. The rich frescoes, the flittering bronze and burnishings, the grand illumination, create such a sensation in the beholder, as he gazes on the magnificent scene of gold and light, that he instinctively thinks of the glory of Solomon's Temple and the story of Aladdin.

Duluth's affluence also infected the community's sports-minded citizens. The first "lake regatta" was held in July 1890 and was, in the words of one participant, attended by "immense crowds [and] except for one drowning accident, the regatta was a

success." The Duluth Curling Club was organized in 1891, and when the club's stones were delivered before its first indoor rink was completed, club members cleared Lake Superior ice on the old outer harbor and held the city's first unofficial bonspiel on Christmas day. The Duluth Driving Park Association opened a race track in Woodland and drew horses and horse race fans from a great distance. The Trysil Ski Club was organized in 1893 and drew its membership largely from the ranks of a local Norwegian men's club.

Education made giant advances in Duluth in the early 1890s. By 1891 public school enrollment was 6,113. That summer ground was broken near the corner of Lake Avenue and Second Street for Central High School, a Romanesque marvel in Minnesota sandstone which cost the taxpayers of Duluth half a million dollars and whose 230-foot clock and bell tower still dominates the city's Central Hillside. In 1892 schools superintendent Robert E. Denfeld launched a campaign to open a "normal school" in Duluth to train teachers for the city's burgeoning school system. Within a decade the Duluth Normal School had its own home at 23rd Avenue East and Fifth Street in a structure which is today part of the University of Minnesota's Duluth campus. Also in 1892, the Sisters of St. Benedict opened a Catholic academy and girls' boarding school, the forerunner of the College of St. Scholastica.

Three major structures rose in downtown Duluth in 1892. The Torrey Building, at 11 stories the city's first skyscraper, was built on Superior Street between Third and Fourth Avenues West. The Union Depot, a fanciful yet utilitarian freight and passenger

Leonidas Merritt, surveyor, timber cruiser, and entrepreneur, spent more than a quarter century pursuing his father's dream of iron riches across the swamps and rocky hillsides of the Minnesota Arrowhead. With his brothers and nephews he finally found the ore in 1890, but lost the deed to financier John D. Rockefeller in the economic panic of 1893. Lost too were their dreams of a family-owned mineral empire. Courtesy, Duluth Public Library

railroad terminal, was erected at Fifth Avenue West and Michigan Street. And on June 25, city fathers and federal bureaucrats laid the cornerstone of a new post office-federal building at Fifth Avenue West and First Street.

A major chapter in Duluth's industrial history was officially opened on July 22, 1893, when the Duluth, Missabe & Northern Railway delivered the first 10 carloads of Mesabi iron to the gargantuan wooden ore docks then being fabricated on St. Louis Bay by the industrious and tireless Merritt family. While the Merritts had been shipping their iron on contract with other railroads over docks in Superior for two years, the shipment of a few hundred tons of iron that warm summer day fulfilled their family dream that their iron enterprise should, in the words of Alfred Merritt, "be a Minnesota road throughout." And while the national economic crash of 1893 caused the family to lose its fabulous iron empire, that shipment was the precursor of more than 1 billion tons of iron which have since flowed over the docks of Duluth to help build the nation and shape the world.

The Zenith City weathered the crash of 1893 far easier than it had two previous economic panics. The city's industrial base had been greatly diversified and continued to expand. By the early 1890s, for example, Duluth lumber mills were cutting and shipping more than 150 million board feet a year. Alger-Smith, Mitchell and McClure, and Merrill and Ring were but three of the firms which constructed giant sawmills and their ancillary docks and storage yards on the waterfront from Rice's Point to Oneota in the last decade of the century. By the end of that decade the city's annual output exceeded 400 million board feet.

In 1894 Duluth opened its doors and opened its hearts to the victims of one of the dreaded, deadly side effects of timber-harvesting prosperity—forest fires. On September 1 flames roared through the small town of Hinckley and several neighboring communities some 75 miles south of the Head of the Lakes. On September 2 Mayor Ray T. Lewis called upon the citizens of Duluth

. . . to provide ways and means for the care of the people who have been left destitute and homeless by the disastrous fire which has burned so many flourishing neighboring towns. Hundreds of men, women, and children were brought to the city last night . . . who have lost their all and are scantily clothed. We must provide food and clothes for them at once. The occasion demands immediate action, and I feel assured that there will be a hearty response to this call.

Duluth's response was just that. Contributors to a "sufferer's relief fund," which read like a who's who of the city's business and

Above left: *All of the players in the Lyceum's pit orchestra were Duluthians. Jens H. Flaaten, fourth from the left in the first row next to his brother, first violinist Gustav Flaaten, emigrated from Norway and became conductor of the Lyceum orchestra at the age of 26. Courtesy, Duluth Public Library*

Top: *Youth members of Duluth's Turnverein pose with their physical education leader, Max Alletzhaeuser. Alletzhaeuser also directed physical education in Duluth schools. Courtesy, Marguerite Lyons*

Bottom: *Varying shades of ivory, cream, orange, and gold decorated the Lyceum Theater's interior. Designed in an Indian style, the theater's boxes were facsimiles of bay windows in Amenhabab, India. All the leading stars of the 1890s performed on its stage, which was one of the largest in the United States. Later it became a movie theater. Courtesy, Northeast Minnesota Historical Center*

social leaders, soon put forward more than $10,000. Churches, hotels, social halls and private homes housed the fire refugees. Within four days the *Duluth News-Tribune* was shouting in headlines, "Eleven hundred sufferers now here—Bring 'em here—There's room for more—Duluth will gladly receive and care for them." The Zenith City's collective heart must truly have helped assuage the tragedy of its neighbors' fiery loss.

While the region's forests fell to the woodsmen's saws and to disastrous fires, another major industry rose out of the waters of Lake Superior. Commercial fishing, which had been practiced a half-century earlier by the American Fur Company, was in the 1890s again helping to feed Duluth and all the Midwest. Major operators included A. Booth and Sons, the Lake Superior Fish Company, and H. Christiansen and Sons. All ran their own boats and also contracted with fishermen from Duluth to Isle Royale, employing literally thousands.

Lake trout was the most plentiful and most favored fish, but those who harvested the water also traded in siskowett, herring and pike. In the late 1890s Duluth fish houses tapped a new market for fresh frozen fish—at least in the winter months—by simply letting nature freeze fresh herring in 100-pound lots, stuffing them into burlap sacks, and shipping them on rail cars to customers from the plains of Illinois to the mountains of Montana. "Frozen with the wiggle in its tail" was the slogan used by one Twin Ports fish merchant to convince buyers of his product's freshness.

While Lake Superior held a limitless supply of fresh water, supplying that water to the ever-increasing population of Duluth was no easy task. For years this responsibility had been left to a private corporation, an arrangement under which, according to one citizen, "the city fared badly. The intake pipes ran too short a distance into the lake, the water became affected by sewage, fever became prevalent, and the people threatened the water company with prosecution because of bad water supply."

In 1898 the city took over the waterworks and spent over $1 million to build a pumphouse and extend intake pipes more than a quarter of a mile into the lake at Lakewood, some nine miles from downtown Duluth. The same citizen then noted, "The generally improved health of the people immediately after the installation of the new water system at once bore testimony to the great improvement that resulted from this new water supply." The water system is still serving Duluth today.

The region was ready to respond when our nation declared war on Spain in 1898. City fathers dispatched Company A of the state militia to St. Paul to be mustered into the United States Volunteer Army. But the 300 Duluth volunteers spent the days of the Spanish-American war at Camp Thomas in Georgia's Chickaugua National Park, battling dysentery instead of the enemy.

On October 13, 1899, Duluth played host for the first time to a sitting president when William McKinley made the Zenith City one of his whistle-stops on a Midwest tour. Most of the city's population turned out to cheer, or at least gawk at, McKinley as he delivered a short, forgettable speech on the steps of Central High School.

As the century turned, the Zenith City of the Unsalted Seas boasted an official population of 52,969, an increase of nearly 60 percent in a single decade. Another indicator of the growth and prosperity evident at the turn of the 20th century was cargo ton-

Architects Emmet S. Palmer and Lucien P. Hall based their design for Duluth's Romanesque Central High School on the Pittsburgh Allegheny Courthouse by famed architect Henry Hobson Richardson. Built of brownstone, the school occupies an entire block on Second Street overlooking the city and lake. Oak, white birch, and sycamore were used in the interior of the building, which now houses the Duluth school administration. Courtesy, Duluth Public Library

Anna Meinhardt was born in Duluth in 1872 on the site of the present Jefferson School. After graduation from Central High, she taught at several Duluth schools and was the principal of Washington Junior High, Salter, and Lakeside schools. Meinhardt served on the Duluth Board of Education from 1940 to 1952. Courtesy, Marguerite Lyons

During the Spanish-American War, Duluth members of the 14th Regiment Minnesota Volunteers were stationed at Camp Thomas, Chickamauga National Park, Georgia, from May until August 1898. Courtesy, Duluth Public Library

Opposite page: The Duluth Aerial Ferry Bridge platform could accommodate six cars for the one minute and 40-second ride. In 1929 the platform was replaced with the movable deck. The bridge has remained a popular tourist attraction as the Aerial Lift Bridge. Courtesy, Northeast Minnesota Historical Center

Commercial fishing on the Great Lakes reached its peak in 1899 when more than 146 million pounds were landed in the United States and Canada. Many of the fishermen along the North Shore prefer to work alone in small boats. Courtesy, Duluth Public Library

nage passing over the docks of the Twin Ports. In 1900 the figure was a record 14,135,237 gross tons, more than a 400 percent increase over 1890. Yet another meter of the city's growth was the salaries paid to municipal officials: The city council agreed to pay Mayor T.W. Hugo $2,500 per year; the city treasurer was paid $2,400, the captain of police $1,400, and the superintendent of streets $840 a year, with horse furnished.

In 1900 the Army Engineers completed a four-year, $7 million improvement project designed to facilitate the mushrooming marine commerce. The Duluth harbor entry had been widened to 300 feet and the canal's wooden dockworks replaced with pre-cast concrete piers which reached some 1,700 feet into the lake. The Duluth press lauded the project as being "of noble proportions, massive yet artistic, and the whole a work that will endure for ages."

While the new canal made it easier for vessels to enter and leave the Duluth harbor, the task of transporting Duluthians across that canal remained a civic headache. City officials had lured the village of Park Point into becoming a part of Duluth in 1890 with a promise to bridge the channel. And while many projects were publicly debated, including proposals to dig a tunnel under the canal rather than build a bridge over it, Minnesota Point residents and visitors alike had to rely on ferryboat service until 1905.

The city of Duluth had okayed construction of a "French patented, suspended, car-transfer bridge" and in 1901 floated $100,000 in municipal bonds for its construction. Engineer C.A.P. Turner designed the span and a contract was let to a consortium of Duluth and Minneapolis business interests. However, this association apparently defaulted and in 1904 the contract was awarded to

the Modern Steel Construction company of Waukesha, Wisconsin.

The contractor poured 730 tons of concrete to anchor the bridge frame on both sides of the ship canal and began raising twin trestleworks which reached 186 feet into the air. As steelworkers bent the frames toward each other hundreds of curious Duluthians gathered daily to see if the structure would topple under its own weight. But all the town cheered the day a huge crane lifted a steel beam into place; men on each outstretched bridge arm slammed rivets in and the unique Duluth Aerial Ferry Bridge stood safely by itself.

That winter a sheet steel car was suspended on wheels which ran atop the span. The car was powered by two gas and electric motors and was equipped with a hand crank in case both failed in mid-passage. The ferry could carry up to 125,000 pounds, rode 13 feet above the water and traveled at a top speed of four miles per hour. Passenger service was inaugurated on March 27, 1905, when a large delegation rode to Park Point and back. The tempestuous Lake Superior did its best to spoil the day, lashing the bridge with driving sleet and winds which shattered several of the car's windows. But the city of Duluth took proud possession of its newest public transit link.

Disaster struck one of the city's other public transportation systems—the incline. On May 28, 1901, fire broke out in a coal bin at the incline's engine house and quickly spread to the Pavilion. One fire company was sent up the incline, fighting its way through smoke and flames which nearly suffocated both men and horses, but the firefighters could do little to quell the blaze. Citizens of Duluth watched from windows and rooftops as flames soon consumed the Pavilion.

Incline engineers realized the peril to their railway and attempted to lash the coach atop the hill to the rails to prevent it from running wild down the grade. But intense heat parted the cables, freeing the massive car for a lightning run to Superior Street. As the *Duluth Herald* reported that afternoon, "Swifter than a Parthian arrow it dashed down the hill—a whirlwind of flame." The vehicle covered the 3,000-foot track in 10 seconds and, as the *Herald* further described:

. . . when the car hit the bottom there was the sound of an explosion. The flames shot up fully 100 feet. The car and station were smashed and thrown clear across the street. Heavy structural steel was twisted and splintered and shattered.

Flaming wreckage was splattered across the rail yards below Superior Street. Miraculously, no one was even injured by the fire or the runaway coach. The incline was repaired and returned to

Duluth's park system is founded on the Boulevard Drive, which skirts the hilltop and passes by picturesque stream gorges, the lakeshore, and its river. Since the Boulevard Drive opened to traffic in 1890, it has been a favorite place to take Duluth visitors. When William Jennings Bryan came to Duluth on a Presidential campaign tour, he said "America has no finer drive than this." Courtesy, Duluth Public Library

Outdoor parties have always been popular in Duluth, despite the short supply of warm days. Duluthians are inordinately fond of their parks and woodlands, so such festivities are common events. Courtesy, Marguerite Lyons

service, now powered by electricity instead of steam. The Pavilion, said the *Herald*, was "in ruins . . . a mass of smouldering ashes"; it was not rebuilt.

A happier event was celebrated on July 4, 1901, when the cornerstone was laid for Duluth's new public library on the corner of First Avenue West and Second Street. The city had had a library association since 1869, but the library had been housed in a number of rented locations. Since the 1890s it had been in the Masonic Temple at Second Avenue East and Superior Street. But with a $75,000 gift from Andrew Carnegie, the city was able to build a home for the library. A focal point of the new structure designed by architect Adolf F. Rudolph, was a Tiffany glass window of the Indian maiden Minnehaha, which had been displayed at the Chicago World's Fair and then donated to the library by Mrs. J.B. Weston of Duluth.

One of the favorite pasttimes of the day for visitors and residents alike was a carriage excursion along Rogers Boulevard, the beginning of today's city-spanning Skyline Parkway. The boulevard was named for W.K. Rogers, the first president of the city's park board who is credited with securing the road's winding route along the crest of Duluth's hills for the public's enjoyment. Then, as now, the parkway offered those who drove it incomparable vistas of the city, of the lake, and of the commerce which joined the two.

Education also continued its advances. The first seven scholars to graduate from the Duluth Normal School received their diplomas in 1903. In 1909 the first structures of the Villa St. Scholastica were built on the college's present Kenwood Avenue campus. A half dozen new elementary schools were built in the first decade of the new century. There also was, for a very few years, a girl's preparatory school called Craggencroft Classical Institute in Hunter's Park.

In 1904 the Work People's College opened in Smithville-Riverside. For the next 35 years the small school would be run by a succession of Finnish-American religious, political, and economic reformers. The college had been established in Minneapolis in 1903 by the Finnish American National Church as a seminary, and

When Hardy School opened in 1892, Director Kate Hardy offered a fine girls' college preparatory education. Designed by Traphagen and Fitzpatrick, the building overlooking Duluth and the lake became Maynard School in 1895, affiliating with the University of Chicago. Later renamed Craggencroft, the school closed in 1902. Courtesy, Duluth Public Library

Children pose with their teacher in the 1890s. In 1880 there were only two or three school buildings in Duluth, but by 1895 there were 32. Courtesy, Marguerite Lyons

The Thomson Dam was constructed by the Great Northern Power Company to replace an old timber dam. Minnesota Power and Light Company took over the operation under lease agreement in 1923 and acquired full ownership in 1927. Courtesy, Duluth Public Library

was moved to Smithville in 1904. From its inception, philosophical differences among its faculty members and its financial backers kept the school in turmoil. The school, whose student body fluctuated from a few dozen to several hundred, served two purposes: to "Americanize" Finnish immigrants and to advocate economic and social reform. In 1909 the college became a Socialist institution, and by 1916 it was closely aligned with the IWW. The school ran sporadically until 1938.

The Zenith City was bathed in new light beginning in 1905 when the Great Northern Power Company constructed a new dam at Thomson on the St. Louis River to tap the river's water-power potential. This wasn't the first scheme to harness the St. Louis above Fond du Lac, but it was definitely the most successful.

Perhaps the grandest plan ever unveiled was that of the Minnesota Canal Company which had in 1883 proposed building a 26-mile canal, 120 feet wide and 20 feet deep, from the St. Louis upstream from Cloquet to the hilltop above Duluth's West End. From there the water would be shot down the hill in huge conduits to turn waterwheels and generate cheap electricity for the city. At $7 million, the project's estimated price tag was anything but cheap. The canal was never built.

When the Great Northern Power Company's project was nearing completion, the *Duluth News-Tribune* would boast that "a water power second in potential to that of Niagara Falls . . . (will be) brought into subjection and harnessed for the uses of the industry of Duluth." The newspaper claimed the Thomson works had the capacity for 200,000 horsepower, although when the first transformer was turned on in 1906 it would draw only 30,000 horsepower, the capacity planned for first-stage development.

1905 also proved to be an eventful year for maritime interests throughout the Great Lakes, particularly in the Twin Ports. Late that November hurricane-force winds ravaged Lake Superior in what some observers have called the lake's worst storm ever. The toll was staggering: 26 vessels damaged or

destroyed, 17 stranded, one foundered. At least 33 lives were lost. And the most spectacular wreck of all occurred right on Duluth's doorstep.

On Tuedsay, November 28, thousands of Duluthians gathered near the ship canal and lined downtown roofs and windows to watch ships challenge the fury of the storm. About 2:15 p.m. the 450-foot, iron-laden steamer *Mataafa* appeared through a snow squall, driving hard for the harbor entry and the protection offered behind Minnesota Point. But just as the giant laker entered the canal it was wracked by the wind and the always troublesome channel currents, its bow struck the north pier, and it was driven back into the lake, slamming broadsides into the pierhead. As the cries of the spectators joined the cry of the wind, the *Mataafa* settled on the bottom less than 150 yards from shore.

The vessel was split amidships, and its cargo bled a rusty red into the mud-brown, white-capped seas. While the crew could be seen signaling from both the fore- and aft-cabins, which were still above water, the intensity of the gale made it impossible for them to launch lifeboats or for the U.S. Life Savers to reach them. Through the night hundreds, at times thousands, of Duluthians stood vigil on the beach, watching as angry seas continuously rolled over the *Mataafa*, driving it ever lower in the water.

In the early morning hours all hope seemed to die when a flickering light which had been burning in the pilot house died. Yet on Wednesday morning—one day before Thanksgiving—the Life Savers reached the broken ship and were pleased to bring 15 of the *Mataafa*'s crew, including its captain, to the safety of shore. They had stayed alive by building a bonfire of hacked-up furniture in a wind-sheltered room in the forward section. But nine men had either drowned or froze to death in the crash which nearly all Duluth had witnessed.

Nevertheless marine commerce continued to expand in the Twin Ports. At the end of the 1907 shipping season Duluthians took it pridefully and yet in stride when it was revealed their harbor had surpassed New York City in gross tonnage handled and had thus become the leading port in the United States.

In the first 20 years of this century new monuments to Duluth's and all the region's prosperity were erected along the city's eastern hillsides and lakeshore. Men who had made or were making their fortunes on the ships, the iron, and the timber—men with names like Alworth, Congdon, Chisholm, Ordean, Dwan, Hartley, Sellwood, Tweed, and Whiteside—built themselves and their families palatial homes. In some cases these homes were estates in the finest European tradition. And Duluth truly was home to a great many men of great money; in the second decade of the 20th century the Zenith City would proudly claim that it had more millionaires per capita than any other American City.

By 1910 Duluth had a recorded population of 78,466. Two years later the citizens of Duluth voted to change their municipal government from the aldermanic to commission form and in the process spawned a bevy of reform-minded commissioners. The five full-time commissioners set out to clean up the streets, bars, and bordellos of the city while expanding police and fire protection.

The biggest single project of the next decade—indeed, the single biggest undertaking in Duluth's history—was launched by the single largest industrial enterprise in our nation. In early 1907 the United States Steel Corporation announced that it would build a major steel production unit in or near Duluth. It was no coincidence that the announcement came at the same time the Minnesota Legislature was debating a bill to impose a double tax on iron ore exported from the state for production into steel. The U.S. Steel project was a carefully devised compromise between the Steel Trust and political leaders in Duluth, on the Iron Ranges and throughout Minnesota which effectively killed the taxation bill and would bring all the Arrowhead, in the words of the *Duluth Herald*, "prosperity of the most brilliant kind."

Steel making was, of course, not new to Duluth. John Shoenberger's Duluth Iron and Steel Company had a blast furnace on Rice's Point as early as 1873. In the 1890s the West Duluth Blast Furnace Company had opened a $1 million facility on the banks of the St. Louis River. In the first years of this century, Captain A.B. Wolvin and other Duluth men of money had acquired and modernized this plant and soon were running a full-scale furnace operation producing some 300,000 tons of pig iron a year and marketing coal, coke, ammonia gas, coal tar, and coal gas. This was indeed a prosperous operation, but it would forever remain in the shadow of the U.S. Steel project.

The U.S. Steel announcement of a $5-6 million project had infected the Zenith City with boundless optimism. One knowledgeable observer predicted that the city's population would skyrocket to 300,000 by 1920 and that U.S. Steel's Minnesota Steel Company plants would be just the beginning of a steel production complex "lining the shores of Lake Superior from Fond du Lac to Two Harbors, and from the Euclid Hotel to Iron River, each striving to outdo its neighbor with smoke and noise." The market for the products of this industrial empire would be the same vast region defined by Thomas Preston Foster four decades earlier.

The Zenith City's euphoria was only slightly diminished when the Duluth Works were not developed as quickly as had been hoped. The first steel would not be rolled out until 1915, by which time the industrial titan had increased its Duluth investment

Pittsburgh Steel Company's John Fritz *loads ore at a West Duluth dock in the 1930s. To load ore, trains run along a high trestle and dump ore into pockets or bins directly under the railroad tracks. Hundreds of chutes move the ore from the pockets into the holds of ships. Courtesy, Duluth Public Library*

Richard Sellwood, son of mining magnate Captain Joseph Sellwood, built his residence at 1931 East Second Street. The Neo-classical home designed by Frederick Kees and Serenus Colburn of Minneapolis has a colonnaded porch and a two-story portico typical of the 1900 look. After Sellwood's death in 1940, the house was donated to the College of St. Scholastica. Courtesy, Duluth Public Library

Minnesota Steel Company's open-hearth furnace building was a monumental addition to Duluth's economy. The company's production facilities included six open-hearth furnaces, by-product coke ovens, and a cement plant. Courtesy, Duluth Public Library

Blast furnaces for the production of structural iron and steel were erected in Duluth as iron ore output increased on the Vermilion and Mesabi Range. The West Duluth Blast Furnace Company was built in the 1890s and later was purchased by Zenith Furnace Company. Courtesy, Duluth Public Library

to more than $20 million. Included in that investment was the development of Morgan Park, a housing project honoring the late J.P. Morgan and intended to meet all the social needs of the steel plant work force.

Construction work at Morgan Park began in the summer of 1913, and the first residents moved in less than a year later. All homes were of poured concrete, cinder block, and timbers. Streets were wide and well-paved; sewer, water, and electrical utilities were all discreetly buried beneath ground. The steel trust also built company offices, an ultra-modern school (which it donated to the Duluth school district), a community club, a general retail building, a company hospital, and two churches (Protestant and Catholic). As only employees of the steel company and its subsidiaries were allowed to live there, there was no doubt that Morgan Park was a company town. It and the industrial complex which made it possible would also earn Duluth a reputation as a company town . . . as U.S. Steel's town.

At about the same time, Duluth was memorializing the man who had first "owned" almost the entire town—Jay Cooke. Descendents of the financier had donated a bronze statue of him to the city, and the monument was placed on a granite pedestal in a small public area at the intersection of Superior Street and London Road, across the street from the newly completed Kitchi Gammi Club, which was yet another symbol of Duluth's affluence.

Halfway through the second decade of the century, Duluth, like much of the nation, was immersed in peaceful prosperity which seemed to have little relation to the war then raging in Europe. Yet that war would change Duluth, as it would change the nation. Nonetheless, many in the Zenith City likely concurred with the editors of the *Duluth Herald* who had declared during the dog days of summer in 1914:

What the war means to us and them [the Europeans] is simple enough: it means that we shall keep out of it, and that we shall go about our business just as though the world were at peace, except that the war in Europe opens up to our farmers, our manufacturers, and our ship-owners a new opportunity to do a great business . . . Let's dedicate our days to the business we have to do, and thus win the prosperity that is our due and the profits that are ours for the grasping.

In 1918 American Architecture *reported that "correct principles of town planning have been followed" in Morgan Park. The monotonous similarity of home design in most company towns was relieved in Morgan Park by variations in gables, eaves, and pitched roofs. Courtesy, Northeast Minnesota Historical Center*

U.S. Steel professed to be interested in its employees, and in this lakeview store building, the company provided shops offering general food, clothing, and barbering, as well as doctors' and dentists' offices. Churches, a community center, and schools were also built. Courtesy, Northeast Minnesota Historical Center

Chapter Five

1916-1945

DAYS OF GLORIOUS EFFORT

By 1916 the nations of Europe had plunged into war, and, as America's hopes for neutrality dimmed, military and industrial preparations were stepped up nationwide. Duluth would indeed profit from the "war to end all wars." All the industries at the Head of the Lakes would boom, and many of the Zenith City's industrialists would reap new riches. But Duluth, like the rest of America, would not be able to stay out of the conflict later known as World War I.

In the summer of 1916 the Duluth unit of the Minnesota National Guard was called up to active duty and was first dispatched to the Mexican border where Pancho Villa was creating an international incident and capturing our national fancy.

When the United States officially entered the war against Germany in April 1917, the Duluth contingent, 1,500 strong, went "over there" as part of the Minnesota Third Infantry. Duluth historian Walter Van Brunt summed up the response at home:

Days which, for soul-stirring, Duluth had never before experienced were frequently recurring, days of glorious effort, personal sacrifice, wonderful achievements in production and resolute administration. All effort was centered on the national effort and purely local development had to be set aside. For instance, the Duluth building record for 1916 was $10,223,598; in 1917, the improvements aggregated only $4,257,913.

In 1932 the Minnesota Steel Company was leased to another U.S. Steel group, the American Steel and Wire Company. Workers at the mill dipped wire in an acid tank before moving it to the wire-drawing machine to be cut. Courtesy, Duluth Public Library

Duluthians could escape from the gnawing worries about World War I at the elegant Rose Garden of the St. Louis Hotel, which replaced the burned Clark House. The sheet music on the piano is a Chauncey Olcott piece from the musical "Heart of Paddy Whack." Courtesy, Duluth Public Library

The U.S. Steel Duluth Works couldn't have timed its opening better to contribute to the Lake Superior region's energetic wartime effort. The first steel ingots were rolled there on December 11, 1915. The Universal Portland Cement Company, another subsidiary, built a $2 million plant alongside the steel mill and used furnace slag to produce some 700 tons of cement daily. In the early 1920s wire and nail mills would be added to the U.S. Steel complex.

In 1916 Alexander McDougall, who at the turn of the century had turned from shipbuilding to other business interests, organized the McDougall-Duluth Company to provide freighters to the friendly nations of Europe. After building two vessels in a small yard at 15th Avenue West and Railroad Street, McDougall and his partners—including Duluthians Julius H. Barnes, Chester Congdon, and Marshall Alworth—moved their operations to a new yard

Duluth Naval recruits pose by the side entrance to the St. Louis County Courthouse during World War I. Two days after America declared war on Germany, seven Minnesota divisions of the Naval Militia were in Duluth, comprised of 22 officers and 326 men. The recruits left for the Navy Yard in Philadelphia with a parade and music to cheer them on their way. Courtesy, Bev Maunu

at Riverside on the St. Louis River.

In addition to building facilities for working on eight vessels at one time, the company also erected apartments and houses for its employees, stores, a small hospital, and a theater. Riverside became the Morgan Park of the Twin Ports shipbuilding industry. During the war period (1916-1921) the McDougall-Duluth yard turned out three dozen steel vessels. All the shipyards of Duluth-Superior contributed 103 vessels to the war effort.

While by autumn 1918 American forces in Europe were buoyed by the prospect of an imminent armistice, Duluthians found themselves besieged by two natural enemies. An epidemic of Spanish influenza was sweeping the nation, and Duluth could not escape. Flu cases mounted daily, and on October 11 Mayor C.R. Magney ordered all public buildings in the city closed indefinitely. Before Magney would lift that order six weeks later nearly 100 would die.

Also that October Duluthians again opened their doors and hearts to the ravaged survivors of fire. Flames, reportedly sparked by a passing train, rolled through the tinder-dry forests and swamps south and west of the lakehead, leveling all in their path. Again, as less than a quarter century earlier, entire towns were destroyed. Included in the holocaust, and suffering the greatest casualties, were Moose Lake and Cloquet. The fire burned to the Zenith City's doorstep; one observer noted, "Duluth's northern boundary was a line of fire." While the flames did invade the city at scattered locations—destroying the Northland Country Club, the Homecroft and Cobb schools, the Alger-Smith lumber yards on Garfield Avenue, and the approaches to the Interstate Bridge— most of Duluth was spared.

Yet more than 1,000 lives were lost in the blaze. Refugees again streamed into Duluth. The armory, churches, schools, and social halls, as well as private residences, were opened to them. Red Cross volunteers, already active and well-organized for the war effort, shifted their attention to succoring the fire's victims. Private relief funds from throughout the western Lake Superior

Henry Schultz (top row, second from left), son of pioneer settler August Schultz, poses with fellow workers by the McDougall-Duluth Shipbuilding Company plant in River-side. During the World Wars a small town grew up around the shipyards, including 60 homes that the company built for its workers. Courtesy, Marguerite Lyons

region soon totaled some $600,000, a figure which did not include the gifts of food, clothing, building materials, and farm stock made available to the refugees. Within a few months a relief commission which had been appointed by Minnesota Governor J.A.A. Burnquist would be able to report, "All who desired were able to return to their land with their stock during the winter."

Duluth celebrated happier times in the winter and spring of 1919. The city welcomed home its war veterans and paid homage to those who would never return. That summer Duluth's first post of the American Legion was founded and named to honor David Gilbert Wisted, the first Duluthian killed in combat on the fields of France. Also in 1919, the Joshua B. Culver Post of the Grand Army of the Republic erected a monument, "Patriotism Guards the Flag," as a tribute to all the city's soldiers and sailors. The statue still stands guard in front of the St. Louis County Courthouse.

While the majority of residents, both individual and corporate, were settling into a peaceful prosperity, one large Duluth industry suddenly found itself high and dry. Adoption of the 18th Amendment to the U.S. Constitution closed the spigots and drained the beer vats of city breweries. Of the three principal breweries — Fitger Brewing, Duluth Brewing and Malting, and People's Brewing — Fitger's was by far the largest and the oldest. The East Superior Street facility could trace its origins to that small brewing house built by the stalwart pioneers of Duluth to counter the harsh economic conditions in 1859. Prior to Prohibition Fitger's had an annual beer output in excess of 150,000 barrels. All three breweries did manage to survive the nation's noble experiment by concocting a wide variety of soft drinks, candies, and cereal beverages, but all quickly reverted to the manufacture of beer and malt liquor when the populace called an end to Prohibition in 1933.

In February 1920 the *Duluth Herald* noted the jubilee of Duluth's incorporation as a city and proudly proclaimed:

Duluth today stands as one of the leading cities of the Northwest, with prospects for the future that are unrivalled. Fifty years of steady growth have resulted in wonderful accomplishments for a city industrially, financially, and from a civic standpoint.

Decennial statistics revealed the Zenith City's growth. Federal census-takers counted 98,917 residents in 1920. Assessed valuation of real and personal property was in excess of $68 million. Bank deposits exceeded $50 million and bank clearings totaled more than $378 million. There were 41 public school buildings valued at $4,355,487; the school levy was nearly $1.25 million, and there were 17,924 pupils in the city's schools. Duluth maintained more than 50 parks and open places and boasted, in a 1921 promotional pamphlet, of "20 miles of well-maintained boulevard, offering a delightful view of the head of Lake Superior."

There were 56 miles of paved streets, 70-plus miles of street railways, and more than 200 miles of sewers. Fourteen railroads had access to the Duluth-Superior waterfront where there were 27.6 miles of improved wharf space. Vessel clearances totaled 9,283, with an aggregate registered tonnage of 35,124,556. Grain elevator capacity was 36.32 million bushels, and grain shipments totaled 62,739,563 bushels; 5,294,576 barrels of flour were also shipped. Iron ore shipments were 33,771,582 tons, not far behind the war-year record of 38 million-plus tons in 1918. And flowing into, rather than out of, the Twin Ports were 9,030,696 tons of coal.

In 1906 the Duluth Boat Club, on Park Point at 10th Street, expanded and built Oatka Branch, giving the club a two-and-a-half-mile watercourse between the two clubhouses. The present Duluth Boat Club facilities are on this Oatka Branch site. Courtesy, Duluth Public Library

Conspicuous by its absence from this listing was any mention of Duluth's lumber industry, as that industry had all but expired by 1920. Walter Van Brunt explained:

The dismantling and removal from Duluth to Canada in 1912 of the old Howard saw mill took from Duluth one of its conspicuous landmarks and emphasized the fact that the "era of lumber" had passed from the Head of the Lakes. The dismantling of the Alger-Smith mill, in 1920, may be looked upon as the interment of the industry that died, as far as Duluth is concerned, with the passing of the Howard plant in 1912.

Despite the city's continued industrial growth, Duluth's history and heritage were sorely blemished on the night of June 15, 1920. A 19-year-old white girl claimed that she had been raped by several young black men, employees of a traveling circus then playing the Zenith City, and police arrested six members of the circus gang. Anger at the very thought of such an abominable act, especially with the racial overtones which were something new to overwhelmingly white Duluth, quickly generated an angry mob which converged on the downtown police station and demanded that the suspects be turned over to the crowd. When police refused, the mob stormed the jail, dragged three of the young men from their cells, and hanged them from a lamppost. Between 5,000 and 10,000 Duluthians participated in, or at least witnessed, the lynch mob's actions.

Yet the ignominy of the triple lynching was quickly supressed by the community, and Duluth roared through the Roaring '20s. Sports captured the city's fancy. The Duluth Boat Club, based in a commodious clubhouse on the bay side of Minnesota Point, consistently produced national championship rowing teams between 1911 and 1923. The glory days for the local oarsmen peaked

in 1922 when Duluthian Walter Hoover won the Philadelphia Gold Challenge Cup and the Diamond Sculls at Henley-on-Thames. (The latter was considered the grandest prize in the world of sculling).

Duluth was also home to one of the charter teams of the National Football League. For most of the 1920s the Duluth Eskimos played under the tutelage of Ole Haugsrud. Perhaps the most famous and talented Eskimo was Ernie Nevers, like Haugsrud a native of Superior, Wisconsin. In 1929 the Eskimo franchise was moved to Orange, New Jersey, and is still playing today as the Washington Redskins.

During this time Duluth was also home to a number of semi-professional and professional hockey teams. In 1928-1929 the Duluth Hornets won the league championship in the newly organized Central Hockey Association. The Hornets played in the Duluth Amphitheater, a 5,000-seat arena built in 1924 at the corner of 12th Avenue East and London Road and proclaimed by the press of the day to be "the most modern artificial ice-skating rink and auditorium in North America." The facility served the region's skating enthusiasts for only 15 years. On February 12, 1939, its snow-laden roof collapsed during intermission at an amateur hockey game. Fortunately, no one was killed or seriously injured, but the amphitheater was never rebuilt.

There was also ample entertainment available for those Duluthians who were not so sports-minded. Radio broadcasting was introduced in the summer of 1922 with station WJAP, a joint venture of the *Duluth Herald*, the Lyceum Theater, and Kelley-Duluth Hardware. The station broadcasted from the Lyceum. The Duluth Playhouse, which today claims the distinction of being the oldest continuing community theater in the nation, was formed in 1914, in the words of its charter, "to stimulate interest in the best drama and to waken the public to the importance of the drama . . . and to work for the social, moral, and educational enhancement of its members." And in 1932 the Duluth Symphony Orchestra was organized and began its tradition of yearly subscription concerts.

The St. Louis County Historical Society was organized in 1922, with William E. Culkin serving as its first president. The Duluth Zoo got its start in 1923 when print shop operator Bert Onsgard sold the city on the idea of supporting a game farm menagerie which he had established at Fairmount Park.

The automobile was also making an indelible impression upon the Zenith City. During the 1920s paved highways were opened from Duluth to the Iron Range, along the North Shore, and to the south toward Minneapolis and St. Paul.

Duluthians and visitors alike enjoyed cruising the waters of the Twin Ports harbor and the St. Louis River. Excursion boats thrived in the first third of this century. None was better known than the *Montauk*, a sidewheel steamer which from May to September during the 1920s and 1930s made two trips a day between downtown and Fond du Lac, ferrying picnickers and pleasure-seekers. The vessel had a large, open deck for dancing and refreshment stands below where, Prohibition notwithstanding, the *Montauk's* crew admitted to dispensing some alcoholic beverages "for medicinal purposes."

Another famous ship arrived at the Head of the Lakes on June 23, 1927, and was greeted by a crowd estimated at 10,000. It was the *Leif Erikson*, a 42-foot replica of the sailing crafts which its namesake is believed to have sailed from Scandinavia to North America nearly 1,000 years ago. The *Erikson* had been built in Korgen, Norway, and, with a crew of five, had retraced the route of the ancient Vikings from Bergen to Boston in 1926. Duluth, some 6,700 miles from the ship's first home, would become its final home in 1929 when Norwegian-American furniture dealer Bert Enger purchased it and donated it to the city to be the centerpiece of a municipal park on the lakeshore at 12th Avenue East.

City fathers took up a new residence in 1928, moving into a City Hall which was built as part of a unified Civic Center at Fifth Avenue West and First Street. A St. Louis County Courthouse had been built there in 1908-1909 by D.H. Burnham, a pioneer city planner who envisioned a classical complex for all government buildings in Duluth. The Civic Center was filled out in 1930 with completion of a new Federal Building and removal of the post office which had stood since 1892.

Duluth was, in many measures, a typical American city. Some critics believe the Zenith City was in fact, so typical that Minnesota novelist Sinclair Lewis used it as the role model for his fictional "Zenith," the setting for his 1922 bestseller, *Babbitt*.

But the pleasant prosperity Duluth enjoyed in the century's early decades was to come to a jolting halt in the 1930s. All the Lake Superior region crashed with Wall Street in October 1929 and, along with the rest of the nation, lapsed into a decade of depression. Within a little more than a year, nearly one-third of the work force of Duluth was unemployed. Indicative of the depths of the Great Depression at the Head of the Lakes are shipping statistics for the two U.S. Steel railroads. (U.S. Steel would not officially merge the Duluth & Iron Range and the Duluth, Mesabi & Northern into the Duluth Missabe & Iron Range Railway until 1938.) In 1929, the D&IR and DM&N carried 27,804,410 tons of iron ore; in 1932 that total plummeted to 1,458,711 tons—the smallest output of Minnesota iron since 1893.

Yet not everything in Duluth was headed down. Large num-

Duluth Boat Club rowers brought fame to the city. Coach James E. Ten Eyck had been one of the world's finest scullers before Julius Barnes hired him for the club in 1911. Under Ten Eyck's guidance the club won 43 national races and dominated the rowing scene from 1913 through 1923. Courtesy, Duluth Public Library

In 1926 the Leif Erikson sailed the route traveled by Viking explorer Leif Erikson, who discovered the North American continent nearly a thousand years ago. Lakeshore Park on London Road at 12th Avenue East was renamed Leif Erikson Park in 1927 and this replica was donated in honor of the Norseman. Courtesy, Duluth Public Library

At the peak of the Great Depression, 8,295 families were on the relief list in St. Louis County. Some were lucky enough to find work in county parks. Courtesy, Duluth Public Library

Northwest Airways established an amphibian base at the old Duluth Boat Clubhouse on Park Point in May 1931. The oarsmen's quarters were turned over to Northwest Airways for office space and a waiting room. Courtesy, Duluth Public Library

bers of Duluthians were looking up at the flying exhibition on the north edge of the city in September 1930 when the Williamson-Johnson Municipal Airport was officially dedicated. A city-owned air facility had been the dream of many civic and business boosters almost since the summer day in 1914 when early aviator Lincoln Beachey had shown the Zenith City its first airplane—a biplane which he crashed into a fence on his first attempted take-off during a demonstration at Athletic Park. The aviator, fortunately, was less seriously injured than his aircraft.

The famed Aerial Bridge was also given a new lift. In the summer of 1929 the ferry car was removed and the bridge truss raised 42 feet. That winter a steel deck was built beneath the truss and counterbalanced by two 485-ton concrete weights. The lift was to be powered by a large battery of electric batteries, although most of the energy required to raise and lower the deck was provided by gravity as the huge concrete slabs alternately rose and fell with the bridge span. The deck rose to a clear height of 135 feet in 55 seconds. Since its inauguration in March 1930 the Duluth Aerial Lift Bridge has risen and fallen thousands of times each year to let commercial vessels and pleasure craft alike enter and leave the port's harbor.

Duluth's banks, like most of the city's inhabitants, weathered the worst of the Depression better than their counterparts in many parts of the nation. Not one bank in the city went under. And when, in March 1933, a national bank holiday was declared, precipitating a debilitating rush on banks elsewhere, the *Duluth Herald* would report:

> Duluthians are taking the national bank holiday in more or less of a carnival spirit and are showing their faith in Duluth institutions by continuing business as usual. Merchants report that business has held up remarkably well during the last few days despite the cessation of banking. Theaters, on the other hand, report a greatly increased business . . . Some merchants report that Duluthians have been very generous in their support, and for the most part have been spending money. The Duluth stores have experienced but a slight decline in business, which is considered nothing when compared to the 50 and 75 percent declines reported in some other cities.

Franklin D. Roosevelt's alphabet soup of federal relief agencies flourished in Duluth and throughout the Minnesota Arrowhead from the mid-1930s until the outbreak of World War II. Chief among these in the Zenith City was the Works Progress Administration. It had been estimated that during its eight-year lifetime the WPA undertook about 450 projects in Duluth with an aggregate payroll in excess of $9.4 million. Two-time Mayor George D. Johnson, who grew to adulthood in Depression-era Duluth, would recall four decades later:

> If you are in Duluth, or have been here within the past 40 years, you have been directly affected by . . . the WPA. Many of Duluth's streets and sidewalks, the airport, water and sewer lines, and most recreation facilities here benefited from the money and physical effort of Harry Hopkins' [administrator of the Federal Emergency Relief Administration] creation of the mid-1930s.

Enger Tower, a gift of Bert J. Enger, was dedicated on June 15, 1939, by Crown Prince Olav of Norway. It is built of native bluestone and has a lookout at each of its six stories. At the top is a beacon that shines over Duluth. Courtesy, Duluth Public Library

The largest single WPA project was the construction of some two miles of storm and sanitary sewers beneath the downtown streets. The sewer line was carved through the city's ancient diabase foundations and measures seven feet high by nearly four feet wide throughout. The most memorable WPA undertaking was the construction of a replica of the early 19th century American Fur company trading post at Fond du Lac. The timber stockade was dedicated as a public park by Mayor S.F. Snively on August 4, 1935.

In 1939 a new landmark rose on Duluth's skyline while an old one was dismantled. On June 15, Crown Prince Olav of Norway dedicated Enger Memorial Tower, a 60-foot octagonal monument built from native Minnesota bluestone and offering panoramic views of the Zenith City and Lake Superior to all who cared to climb its stairs. The memorial pays homage to Bert J. Enger, a native Norwegian whose life in Duluth was the fulfillment of the American Dream. Enger came to Duluth as a young man, went to work in a furniture store, and eventually became head of his own eminently successful store. His fortune grew through real estate and shipyard investments, and at his death Enger willed a major portion of his estate to the city of Duluth. The bronze plaque at the base of the tower commemorates Enger's generosity:

> From common laborer to merchant prince, he demonstrated in his own life that America is a land of opportunity for the immigrant and that her civilization is enriched by his citizenship. In his lifetime, by a very generous gift, he enabled the city of Duluth to acquire and develop the land adjacent to this tower as a park and golf course for the enjoyment of future generations, and at his death bequeathed two-thirds of his estate to the people of Duluth.

On Labor Day 1939 the incline railroad climbed the city's hills for the last time. The Duluth-Superior Transit Company had

On Labor Day 1939 the incline ended its service and was razed for scrap iron. Duluth mourned the loss of its favorite transportation system as the Duluth-Superior Transit Company replaced trolley cars with buses. Courtesy, Duluth Public Library

Mayor Samuel F. Snively, who served from 1921 to 1937, posed with several public officials in 1921. From left to right are Finance Commissioner Leonidas Merritt; Public Commissioner William F. Munian; Public Utilities Commissioner Peter Philip; and Public Works Commissioner James Farrell. Courtesy, Duluth Public Library

found the incline antiquated and costly to maintain; besides, its services were fast being replaced by bus routes from residential neighborhoods to the business district. In the late 1930s transit company general manager Robert B. Thomson inspected the incline's cables daily, counting broken strands to determine if the system was still safe to operate. The announcement of the tramway's abandonment was met by shouts of protest from Duluth residents and railway enthusiasts around the nation. But that autumn it was quickly dismantled, yielding some 2,000 tons of scrap.

The scrap which had been the incline was no doubt used to help supply and arm the forces that were to become the Allied armies in Europe. The war in Europe would, in fact, pull Duluth and all America out of the last grips of the Great Depression.

By 1940, the Head of the Lakes was once again booming. U.S. Steel's Duluth Works, which had shut down its furnaces completely in the mid-1930s, was working round the clock. Record tonnages of iron again passed through the docks of the Twin Ports. Many firms won defense contracts which would pump hundreds of millions into the region's economy. Richard L. Griggs, president of Northern National Bank, would sum up the city's ambivalence toward its renewed prosperity: "Undoubtedly, 1940 has seen the backbone broken of what may be regarded as America's longest and greatest depression. . . . We would be happy indeed if prosperity were based upon a sound basis of peace production rather than the very ugly business of war."

S.F. Snively

S.F. Snively spent more time as mayor than anyone else in the history of Duluth, and during his 16-year tenure he would see the Zenith City both buoyed by prosperity and wracked by the gloom of depression.

Samuel Frisbee Snively was born November 24, 1859, in the Cumberland Valley of Pennsylvania. He could trace his American ancestry to the earliest days of William Penn's proprietorship of that commonwealth and would point with pride to the fact that four of his forebears had fought in the American Revolution and his father and an uncle had served in the Union Army during the Civil War. He was educated in Pennsylvania common schools and attended Dickinson College in Carlisle, Pennsylvania. In 1883 he entered the Philadelphia law office of Benjamin Harris Brewster, then attorney general of the United States. In 1885 he earned a law degree from the University of Philadelphia.

Snively moved to Duluth in 1886 and began what proved to be a very lucrative law practice. But he apparently lost all he had in what he termed "the financial massacre of 1893" and sometime thereafter joined the gold rush to the Klondike. In Alaska he reportedly made another fortune, but again lost it before he returned to Duluth for good. He went into the real estate business with J.L. Washburn and John G. Williams, acquiring and selling large tracts of railroad land grant property in northeastern Minnesota and northwestern Wisconsin.

In 1921, in his second bid for municipal office, Snively was elected mayor of Duluth. He was re-elected in 1925, 1929, and 1933 and so presided over the city during the heady days of the Roaring '20s and the darkest nights of the Depression 30s. Under the commission form of municipal government the mayor was principally a figurehead, yet Snively figured he could do much for the betterment of Duluth and worked with the energy of a dozen men.

Mayor Snively championed improvements in the city's extensive network of public parks. And he worked tirelessly to extend the famous Skyline Boulevard. He spent much of his time—he remained a lifelong bachelor—in the parks and along Duluth's rocky, wood-covered hillsides and financed some of his favorite projects with his own money. He donated 150 acres to the city through which Snively Parkway now meanders, and he proudly oversaw completion of the boulevard from Fond du Lac to Lester River in 1934.

At age 77, Snively sought re-election to a fifth term as mayor. Although his popularity among the citizens of the Zenith City had waned but little, he was defeated by C. Rudolph Berghult, at 32 the youngest mayor then elected in Duluth and the city's first native-born chief executive. However, Snively continued to serve the public, being employed as a part-time city parks supervisor until his death on November 7, 1952.

S.F. Snively might well have written his own epitaph in an autobiographical sketch for a 1932 book, *Who's Who in St. Louis County:*

My life here in Duluth, like that of many of my contemporaries, has had its successes and its disappointments, but was always lived in support of measures I believed designed for the common good of this city and its people.

Four of Duluth's mayors were (left to right): C.R. Berghult, W. Prince, C.R. Magney, and Samuel F. Snively. Courtesy, Duluth Public Library

Mayor Samuel F. Snively helps plant seedlings at Brighton Beach near Congdon Boulevard. Courtesy, Duluth Public Library

Prosperity was on the horizon for Duluth by 1940. Defense contracts went to Marine Iron and Shipbuilding Company, Coolerator, Clyde Iron Works, Klearflax Linen Looms, and other firms. Through Duluth's "glorious effort," the city grew and prospered during the war. Courtesy, Duluth Public Library

Duluth's recorded population in 1940 was 101,065. (The 1930 federal census had recorded 101,463 residents, far below the unofficial estimates of more than 112,000 persons who had called Duluth home shortly before the crash of 1929.) Of the 1940 number, nearly 2,000 had enlisted in or had been drafted into the U.S. armed services before December 6, 1941. Two Duluth servicemen were among those killed in the Japanese attack on Pearl Harbor. In all, nearly 16,000 Duluthians would serve during the war; some 600 would die.

Besides the immeasurable contributions of the men and women who served in the armed forces, the biggest contribution the Twin Ports would make to the Allied war effort would be, as in World War I, the production of ships. Shipbuilding in Duluth and Superior had virtually ceased after World War I. But between 1940 and 1945, seven reactivated or newly activated yards would send 191 steel vessels down the ways and down the lakes.

Julius H. Barnes, who headed the Barnes-Duluth Shipbuilding Company (which succeeded McDougall-Duluth at Riverside), took to the task with particular fervor. The vessel *Robert L. Barnes*, the first ship launched by McDougall-Duluth in 1916, was still in service to the Navy and had been captured in the Pacific by the Japanese at the outbreak of the war. Julius Barnes was intent upon avenging the affront to his shipyard and to his family name.

Duluthians at home rolled up their sleeves and shrugged off the adversities which warfare imposed. They took rationing—first sugar, then rubber, then gasoline, and then meat, coffee, and dairy products—in stride. They gave to all sorts of drives—scrap iron, paper, even silk. And when Uncle Sam sold war bonds, Duluthians continually oversubscribed, as they had during World War I. By war's end the citizens of Duluth had purchased more than $150 million of these bonds. Brownouts, blackouts and air raid drills

became routine, although the fear and uncertainty which seized the nation never did.

When, in May 1945, Harry Truman proudly announced victory in Europe, the *Duluth News-Tribune* observed:

Duluth yesterday just didn't have the spirit left for a final spontaneous outburst. President Truman's official proclamation of VE-Day came merely as a signal for prayer and thanksgiving and the re-dedication to achieve victory in the Pacific as speedily as possible.

And when, on August 15, 1945, President Truman announced the surrender of Japan, Mayor George W. Johnson announced there would be no formal civic celebration in the Zenith City; rather he urged all citizens to peacefully "pay homage to those who so gallantly gave their lives for this day." But Duluthians did celebrate. The *News-Tribune* reported:

Unrestrained joy, bordering on hysteria, gripped Duluth last night as thousands swarmed the downtown area to celebrate the return of peace . . . Adults and bobby-sockers alike shook sleigh bells, threw hats in the air, and flung rolls of paper out of car windows. Despite the fervor, people seemed to be half-tenderly keeping an eye on each other . . .

The following morning the newspaper stated: "Duluth with the rest of the nation will be going back to 'business as usual' today, although the slowly accelerating peacetime activity still will be held up in spots." But no one in Duluth or anywhere else really knew what would thereafter constitute "business as usual."

Julius Barnes took over the McDougall shipyards in Riverside and acquired a government contract for building tankers. The first tanker was launched the next year. Forty-five ships were built at Barnes' Riverside yard from 1942 to 1945. Courtesy, Duluth Public Library

Chapter Six

1946-Present

PATHWAYS TO THE FUTURE

The Zenith City hardly shifted gears to adjust to "the slowly accelerating peacetime activity" following the war. Servicemen returning home for the most part found jobs—often well-paying—waiting for them. Many were jobs which for the past four years had been held by their sisters, their wives, or their mothers. Shipping statistics for U.S. Steel's Duluth, Missabe & Iron Range Railway again bore witness to the health of the region's economy. Between 1946 and 1953, iron tonnages on the DM&IR averaged more than 40 million per year and set an all-time record of 49.32 million tons in 1953. That year, steel production at the Duluth Works totaled 918,000 tons.

Many servicemen came home intent upon better educating themselves. And Duluth was prepared to serve them. For several years civic and business leaders had been lobbying the University of Minnesota to establish a broad-based, four-year institution at the lakehead. (Duluth State Teachers College had succeeded the Duluth Normal School in 1921 and did offer a four-year curriculum, but only in education.) In 1946 University President James Morrill endorsed the concept, and the following February he and Duluth Regent Richard L. Griggs persuaded the University's Board of Regents to establish its first branch campus in Duluth. The University of Minnesota-Duluth took up residence in the same building which had housed Duluth Normal's first class.

The East Hillside campus soon proved too small and university officials looked eagerly for room to grow. A 160-acre, tax-forfeit tract was identified just six blocks north of the old campus, and in 1948 Griggs himself purchased the property and donated it

Taconite is transported from mines to ore ships by the Duluth, Missabe, and Iron Range Railroad, one of the nation's major ore carriers.
The history of the DM & IR has paralleled the history of the ore industry in Minnesota.
Courtesy, Duluth, Missabe, and Iron Range Railroad

These Navy Reserve Seabees (Construction Battalion) come from Minnesota, Wisconsin, and Michigan. Stationed at the Duluth Naval Reserve base on Park Point, they are a service group working under the command of SWCM Bill Moraski on projects such as children's camps. Courtesy, Naval Reserve

to the university. That fall ground was broken for the first building on campus. By 1951 UMD had an enrollment of 1,208, a teaching staff of 123, and offered its students more than 700 classes.

In 1950, Duluth's recorded population was 104,511. The city's dozen banks had deposits in excess of $166 million; 1,750 retail outlets did more than $143 million in business while 225 wholesale houses posted sales of nearly $200 million. And in terms of gross tonnage, the Duluth-Superior harbor still ranked second in the nation, trailing only New York City.

Military reserve and National Guard units became active in the community. The largest and most energetic of Duluth's reserve contingents was the 179th Fighter Interceptor Squadron, Minnesota Air National Guard, which found a home at the Duluth airport. In 1951 the 179th was joined by the 515th Air Defense Command of the United States Air Force. The *Duluth Herald* described what the arrival of the regular Air Force would mean to the Head of the Lakes:

Duluth's large airport will grow even bigger in 1952. This year's construction will place it among the world's leading airports . . . [The] biggest reason for its rapid expansion is national defense. Duluth is strategically located astride a possible invasion route. The city's vital industries would be logical targets, too. Therefore, the Defense Department is spending about $10 million to build the base into a formidable air bastion.

One of the new vital industries in the region in the early 1950s was petroleum refining and shipping. Refineries were built at Superior and at Wrensall, some 25 miles south of Duluth, and connected to Canadian and Gulf Coast oil fields by continent-spanning pipelines. The products of these refineries were sent down the Great Lakes in a fleet of small tankers to fuel Midwest markets.

Taconite was another major industry emerging in the Minnesota Arrowhead. Taconite is a low-grade iron ore whose presence had long been known but dismissed by iron men as long as the seemingly endless reserves of rich natural ore fed the nation's steel mills. But World War II had seriously depleted those reserves. In 1951, Reserve Mining Company and Erie Mining Company unveiled two mammoth commercial projects to refine the taconite ore and make it competitive with natural iron.

Emery D. Hoensheller, industrial director of the Duluth Chamber of Commerce, lauded these developments: "Taconite alone will eventually mean an area investment of $500 million and three times as many mining jobs as now." However, E.W. Davis, who had experimented with taconite production for a third of a century and was closely allied with the Reserve Mining project, would recall that even in the early 1950s some of the Zenith City's movers and shakers were still shaking their heads skeptically over taconite:

Many Duluth mining men were openly skeptical of such a large and risky investment. As more and more information was released about the project, Reserve men received cooler and cooler receptions as they passed through Duluth. The ribbing at the Kitchi Gammi Club, a meeting place for business and professional men of the area, became sharper and at times almost insulting.

Yet by the time the first boatload of processed taconite headed down the lakes from Reserve's Silver Bay plant in the spring of 1956, nearly all skepticism had been erased.

One of Duluth's social institutions of the post-war period was

Duluth has one of the largest per capita park and municipal areas in America. One of its most outstanding recreational areas is Minnesota Point (Park Point) beach, photographed here in the 1930s. Courtesy, Duluth Public Library

Lake Superior
Park Point.

an unassuming old gentleman named Albert Woolson. He had been born nearly a decade before the Reverend Joseph Wilson found a name for the frontier settlement of Duluth, and had taken up residence in the Zenith City in 1905, some 40 years after he had served in the Grand Army of the Republic. Woolson outlived all the legions of the Union Army and for the last several years of his life, until his death at age 109 in 1956, was a fixture at all public observances of Armistice and Memorial days. Most of a generation of young Duluthians grew up with Albert Woolson as the featured attraction of their schools' patriotism programs.

The voters of Duluth decided to once again change their form of municipal government in 1956, replacing the five-member commission with a strong mayor-council system. That year Eugene Lambert beat incumbent Mayor George D. Johnson for the city's top office, although Johnson would return to the mayor's office for five years in the mid-1960s.

Commercial television made its debut in Duluth in 1953. Dalton A. LeMasurier, president and general manager of station KDAL, described the new medium as "the most potent social, economic, and political force the nation had known." Within two years Duluthians would be able to choose between two local outlets to serve the fast-growing American addiction to the new medium.

For citizens and visitors who relished their leisure time out of doors, Minnesota Point was still a favored haven. The city had acquired a 200-acre tract on the far end of the promontory in 1936 and, with the help of WPA funds and work forces, had developed the site into a popular recreation-amusement center. Docks for pleasure craft, a bathhouse, picnic areas, baseball fields, and horseshoe courts were complemented by a small collection of city-owned or city-leased amusement rides. But the main attraction was, and still is, the amber-sand beach on the Lake Superior side of the point. The anonymous authors of the Work Projects Administration Writers' Program in Minnesota had in 1941 focused on this beach and perpetuated a bit of local folklore about which hardy and resolute residents still take pride: "Duluthians prefer to swim on cloudy, windy days, and like best to go in during or soon

after a northeaster; though the atmosphere may be cool, the wind will have carried the warmer surface water in shore."

The 1950s also saw fulfillment of a centuries-old dream which had been fostered by the men who chose to live and trade along the 2,000-mile-plus North American inland waterway. A joint U.S.-Canadian St. Lawrence Seaway was officially opened in 1959, linking the Head of the Lakes directly with the Atlantic Ocean—indeed, with all the world.

The first attempt to make it possible for marine traffic to pass from salt water to fresh had occurred in 1689—just one decade after Daniel Greysolon visited the western tip of the Great Lakes—when the Society of Jesus began to cut a shallow canal around the Lachine Rapids at Montreal. By the 1850s small vessels were able to make their way all the way from Lake Superior to the Atlantic via the Soo Locks, Canada's Welland Canal and the St. Lawrence River. For the next century a succession of national and international waterway commissions put forward a succession of proposals for a major all-water route. Some followed the St. Lawrence, others the route of the Erie Canal and the Hudson River to New York City. All would have required huge outlays of money—much of it public money—and all failed to win the approval of the U.S. government.

Albert Woolson settled in Waseca, Minnesota, in 1862 and came to Duluth in 1905. He enlisted in the Union Army in 1864 when he was only 17 years old, and as a drum major, he took part in Sherman's march to the sea. He was the last surviving Union Army member. Courtesy, Northeast Minnesota Historical Center

Julius Barnes brought this plane to Duluth during the annual Lark O' the Lake festivities in 1913 as a tourist promotion. Lark O' the Lake occurred in July and August and included a variety of entertainments, some held at the Duluth Boat Club. Courtesy, Marguerite Lyons

Excursion rides around the harbor allow visitors to view the Aerial Lift Bridge, ore docks, grain elevators, foreign ships, and the world's largest coal docks. Courtesy, Duluth Convention and Visitors Bureau

All, that is, until the Canadian government announced in 1953 that it would proceed with a St. Lawrence waterway and hydro power project with or without the United States as its partner. Congress almost immediately voted to join Canada. In 1954 President Dwight Eisenhower tapped Lewis G. Castle, a former Duluth bank president and civic leader, to be the first administrator of the St. Lawrence Seaway Development Corporation. During the next five years the corporation and its Canadian counterpart undertook one of the biggest maritime construction projects in all history.

At the Head of the Lakes the public Seaway Port Authority of Duluth was organized. With $10 million—$5 million from the state of Minnesota, $4 million from St. Louis County, and $1 million from the city of Duluth—the authority constructed the Clure Public Marine Terminal on the Superior Bay side of Rice's Point. The terminal would boast berthing for nine ships, two 90-ton gantry cranes, on-site rail service, a tank farm, and refrigerated storage and warehouse space. The facility, billed as "Minnesota's Gateway to the World," was ready for the commerce of the world when the seaway opened in April 1959, Kenneth Duncan, first chairman of the Duluth port authority, gave voice to new visions for the Zenith City:

> There is no reason why the multitudinous imports now made from the docks of New York, New Orleans, and San Francisco should not come into Duluth for distribution to our trade area. We have the facilities, the labor pool, and the transportation system.

While major import business did not immediately materialize (imports still represent a minor portion of the Twin Ports' commerce) the St. Lawrence Seaway nonetheless brought new prosperity to Duluth. In 1959, 1.99 million tons of export trade, most of it grain and grain products, flowed through Duluth and Superior. The following year the export figure had risen to 2.43 million tons.

The population of Duluth reached its peak in 1960 with 106,884 residents. The city's economy continued to be reflected by cargo tonnages passing through the harbor—that year a healthy 42.68 million gross tons. Forest industries were also enjoying a revival in the western Lake Superior region, although the focus was now on pulp wood and paper production rather than pine lumber.

And a new industry—actually, an old industry whose economic importance was at last being widely recognized—also emerged in the early 1960s. That industry was tourism. As the *Duluth News-Tribune* stated in describing the formation of the Duluth Convention and Visitors Bureau in 1960, "Prospectors in the Head of the Lakes area have joined a gold rush. They're looking for part of a $4 billion bonanza in lapel pins." The bureau hoped to attract people to Duluth to mingle their business conventions with the pleasure of the region's scenic attractions. Those attractions were also being ever more eagerly promoted by the Minnesota Arrowhead Association and Duluth's Chamber of Commerce.

The tourism and business promoters found a somewhat unconventional ally for their campaigns in organized labor. Labor federations—craft shops and trade unions—had been active in the Zenith City almost since its founding. Organized labor had a long and generally admirable history as a dominant force in Duluth, and in all of northeastern Minnesota. In the second half of this century Duluth's labor organizations would be at the forefront of many political, civic, and social issues not usually associated with organized labor. They worked for tax breaks to encourage industrial expansion; the 1964 Minnesota Taconite Amendment, which spurred that industry and helped revitalize all the Arrowhead, likely could not have passed without labor's support, and they lobbied for city charter changes and school bonding referendums.

In 1965 Gerald W. Heaney, a Duluth attorney and long-time activist in Minnesota's Democratic-Farmer-Labor Party, summed up labor's philosophy:

I think it is fair to state that any employer who moves to northeastern Minnesota can expect to find a hard-working, well-educated labor movement that is willing to give a full day's work for a fair day's pay, but will insist on its full democratic rights to bargain collectively and to be an effective and meaningful force in the community. In the long run, this means a good community.

Education continued to advance, and the community's colleges continued to grow. In 1964 UMD had an enrollment of more than 3,200, and university officials were planning building programs estimated at $17.7 million in the next 10 years. By the end of the decade, enrollment would top 5,000. Major building projects were also undertaken at the College of St. Scholastica, which in 1965 had some 500 women students. The school went coed in 1970, when the first 50 male students were admitted. The vital link between these colleges and the community's long-term economic well-being was defined by UMD Provost Raymond Darland in 1965:

It will be today's youth . . . if we can retain them in our area—who will determine just how important the three T's—timber, taconite, and tourism—are to be in northeastern Minnesota.

A sizeable segment of Duluth's past gave way for its future in the early 1960s. The Gateway Urban Renewal Project, a federally-inspired and largely federally-funded redevelopment effort, razed nearly all structures on a 10-acre tract at the western end of the downtown business district. Two landmarks, the once-grand Lyceum Theater and the aging yet elegant Spalding Hotel, fell in this assault on urban decay. Also leveled was Duluth's bowery. But the denizens of the district's flophouses, taverns and low-cost eateries didn't vacate the city; they simply established conclaves in business neighborhoods just east and north of their old haunts.

The importance of Lake Superior to all the region was re-emphasized in 1965 with the announcement that the federal government would construct a $2.5 million National Water Quality Standards Laboratory on the lakeshore near the Lester River. The facility would pioneer in aquatic-environmental research; some of its staff would play major roles in the decade-long Reserve Mining Company pollution trial. On another lake front, commercial fishing was enjoying a revival as scientists found methods to extermi-

Light and color accentuate the block-long new library. On the top floor is the wood-paneled North Shore Room, which houses reference and adult nonfiction areas. The Superior Street side has the children's area and the Popular Library. Administrative offices and meeting rooms are on the lower level. A Media Center provides facilities for watching films. Photo by Jeff Frey

nate the sea lamprey, a blood-sucking eel which had nearly eliminated many fish species in the lake.

All the Lake Superior region celebrated with the Zenith City in August 1966 when the Duluth Arena-Auditorium was officially opened amid cheers of "Hello, World." The $6.1 million complex on the waterfront below downtown included a 5,600-seat arena and a 2,300-seat auditorium-theater which provided the Twin Ports with an entertainment and convention headquarters that had been sorely absent since the Pavilion burned 65 years earlier.

Minnesota's most popular and successful favorite son, Vice President Hubert H. Humphrey, lauded the foresight of the citizens of Duluth who had voted their tax dollars to make the Arena-Auditorium a public dream-come-true: "You were not concerned with the possibility of a 'white elephant.' You were concerned with doing something about the future of your community . . . I would say you made a good investment." In its first five years, more than 3 million people would pass through the Arena-Auditorium's turnstiles.

One of the principal forces behind the Arena project was a man Humphrey described as "my very good friend Jeno Paulucci." Jeno F. Paulucci was and is possibly the most flamboyant and successful figure in 20th century Duluth. His career has been the stuff of Horatio Alger. He is a native of Minnesota's Mesabi Range, the son of working-class Italian immigrant parents. In the mid-1940s he founded the Chun King Corporation in Duluth with a $2,500 loan and endless ambition; 20 years later he sold the firm for $63 million.

He then founded Jeno's Inc. in Duluth, which is today one of the nation's leading producers of frozen pizza, hot snacks, and convenience foods. Paulucci has invested millions of dollars and immeasurable time and energy in projects and programs to better the economic condition of Duluth and all northeastern Minnesota. His philanthropic efforts have enriched both the citizens and the culture of his home. In his own words, "Yesterday's best is already old; only tomorrow's is new."

The Zenith City was gaining new recognition for its role in fostering and preserving the health of citizens throughout western

The St. Louis County Heritage and Arts Center is located in the Depot, designed by the Boston firm of Robert Swain Peabody and John Goddard Stearns. The architects presented Duluth with a chateau-like brick, sandstone, and granite building, which is listed on the National Register of Historic Places. Courtesy, the Depot

Lake Superior. As the *Duluth News-Tribune* explained in 1970: "In the world of medical care, Duluth is a metropolitan center. Its hospitals and highly regarded professionals draw patients from throughout northern Minnesota, Wisconsin, and Michigan, and from parts of Canada as well." In 1969, both St. Luke's and St. Mary's hospitals had completed major expansion projects.

Miller Memorial (now Miller-Dwan) Hospital, which had been founded as a facility to serve "worthy poor and sick" by a bequest from former Mayor A.M. Miller, was, in 1970, constructing a 200-bed addition and would soon offer specialized treatment for burn victims and patients dependent on chemical treatment. The three hospitals employed more than 2,000 persons, making health care one of the city's largest industries. And in the early 1970s, the University of Minnesota opened a family practices medical school at its Duluth campus.

Yet during the 1960s Duluth's population was growing both older and smaller. The most ambitious construction projects of the period were for residential complexes for the elderly. And, in 1970, city officials launched a concerted census registration campaign to push the decennial federal head count a hairbreadth above the 100,000 figure.

In late 1971 U.S. Steel Corporation announced the phasing-out of its Duluth Works. Because of stringent new state environmental protection laws, U.S. Steel would have faced major new expenditures to keep its Duluth plant open. The corporation decided instead to close its blast furnace because of, in the words of U.S. Steel Chairman Edwin Gott, "the absence of a steel market in this area of sufficient size to provide both the volume of business and the economic potential necessary to justify a large investment for a modern, integrated steel production unit." Less than two years later U.S. Steel announced the closing of its cold-side production units. And, in 1975, it ceased operations at its Duluth

cement plant. The city's largest employer had closed shop.

A happier event was celebrated on the hillsides behind the former U.S. Steel plant in December 1974. That month Spirit Mountain, a $6.55 million, 900-acre recreation area, was dedicated. The mountain, in which the taxpayers of Duluth had invested some $3 million, is a city-owned and city-operated facility intended to tap the burgeoning winter recreation and tourism market. It has a dozen alpine slopes, chair lifts, a chalet, cross-country ski trails, and camping and picnic grounds. Manley Goldfine, first chairman of the citizen Spirit Mountain Authority, optimistically predicted, "Spirit Mountain will be the best of all worlds for Duluth. The recreation will be greatly enjoyed by everyone in the area. It will improve business, especially in the winter, and it will create jobs."

The Zenith City experienced a cultural and historical renaissance in the second half of the 1970s. In 1976 the Twin Ports, like the rest of the United States, was infected with euphoric retrospection as the nation noted its bicentennial. The most memorable event in a summer of public celebrations was the visit of the three-masted Norwegian sailing vessel *Christian Radich;* thousands upon thousands of people queued up on the dock in front of the Arena-Auditorium just to have the chance to walk across the tall ship's deck. Three years later Duluth again embarked on a summer of festivities to commemorate the tercentenary of Daniel Greysolon's first visit to the Head of the Lakes. In the interim, city fathers and civic leaders had established a formal "sister city" relationship with Saint Germain-Laval, the ancient French village which was the birthplace of Sieur du Lhut.

The Depot—properly the St. Louis County Heritage and Arts Center—opened its doors in the picturesque old Union Depot at Fifth Avenue West and Michigan Street in May 1977. The center brings under one roof nearly a dozen of the community's cultural

Trolley cars, sponsored by the Lake Superior Museum of Transportation, carry passengers past the recreated Duluth storefronts in Depot Square. Courtesy, the Depot

organizations, including the St. Louis County Historical Society, the A.M. Chisholm Museum, the Duluth Playhouse, and the Duluth-Superior Symphony Association. A focal point of the Depot has become the Lake Superior Museum of Transportation, one of the nation's largest collections of historical railroad equipment. And like many of the Depot's displays, the museum presents a hands-on exhibit—railroad buffs of all ages can climb aboard many of the trains housed there. Kay Slack, first president of the Depot Board of Directors, summed up the center's philosophy: "We're not a fine arts facility . . . we're a people's art facility."

And in June 1980 the city dedicated its new public library across Michigan Street from the Depot. The $6.8 million library, into which architect Gunnar Birkerts instilled a modernistic sense of the city's proud maritime heritage, is intended to serve Duluth-ians well into the 21st century.

On the waterfront, the Seaway Port Authority in 1979 totalled gross cargo tonnages handled in the Twin Ports since the St. Lawrence Seaway had opened two decades earlier. The 20-year aggregate of more than 780 million tons was truly phenomenal.

In early 1980 the U.S. Air Force announced that it would abandon its entire mission in Duluth. The closure included the SAGE (semi-automatic ground environment) control center, which in its heyday housed the brains of the Pentagon's missile guidance and missile tracking network. City officials estimated the departure of the Air Force would cost Duluth more than $30 million a year in lost wages and lost business.

Duluth's population in 1980 was counted at 92,811, a figure arrived at after the city filed suit against the U.S. Census Bureau

Above: *Margaret Culkin Banning, one of the most prolific and successful 20th-century American authors, spent most of her life in Duluth. In addition to writing more than 40 novels during her 60-year career, Banning traveled widely and was active in myriad civic and social activities in the Zenith City until shortly before her death in early 1982. Courtesy, Duluth Public Library*

Margaret Culkin Banning

Margaret Culkin Banning was an inveterate observer of human society and a prolific chronicler of what she observed. She truly was a citizen of the world; she also was a nearly life-long citizen of Duluth.

Margaret Culkin Banning was for six decades among the most prolific of American novelists and essayists. She was born in the small Minnesota farm town of Buffalo in 1891. Her family moved to Duluth shortly before the turn of the century when her father, William E. Culkin, was named register of the northeastern Minnesota federal land office. She was educated in the Duluth public schools and at the Convent of the Sacred Heart in Rochester, New York. In 1912 she graduated Phi Beta Kappa from Vassar College and a year later received a certificate in social work from the Chicago School of Civics and Philanthropy.

In 1914 she married attorney Archibald T. Banning in Duluth. They had four children and traveled extensively in this country and in Europe. Amid the travels and the child-rearing, Mrs. Banning published her first novel, *Marrying*, in 1920. The book marked the beginning of a lifetime of writing, a lifetime which would include 39 books and more than 400 magazine articles and essays, many published in the most popular and most prestigious periodicals of their day. Her writing embodied her social values and those of the societies which she observed around her at home and in her broad travels. Much of her work dealt with issues considered to be in the vanguard of social thought and social activism.

The Bannings' marriage ended in divorce in 1930. In 1944 Margaret Culkin Banning married LeRoy Salsich, president of U.S. Steel's subsidiary, Oliver Iron Mining Company. She retained the Banning name for her professional career.

Margaret and LeRoy Salsich kept homes in Duluth, New York City, and Tryon, North Carolina. During the 1930s, 1940s, and 1950s she was active in a wide range of civic and social affairs in Duluth and in Republican politics in Minnesota. She was long a champion of Duluth's public library, and during the Second World War was a member of the Advisory Committee of the Writers' War Board and spearheaded war bond sales campaigns in the Head of the Lakes region. In 1934 she was named to the Duluth Hall of Fame, the first woman to be accorded that honor. The Zenith City again paid homage to her in 1969 when Mayor Ben Boo proclaimed May 21 "Margaret Culkin Banning Day," commemorating her national and international literary accomplishments and her hometown civic contributions, as well as the publication of her 31st novel, *Mesabi*.

In the late 1970s she sold her Duluth home and settled for good in North Carolina. She did, however, return regularly to the Lake Superior region. She died in Tryon on January 4, 1982, while working on yet another novel. A dozen years earlier Margaret Culkin Banning Salsich had explained to a magazine writer why, after all her travels, she continued to come home to Duluth: "I love Duluth. The atmosphere, the scenery, the air, the people. And, of course, my roots are here. This is where I want to be."

Northern Pacific's first locomotive, the wood-burning Minnetonka, *belongs to the collections of the Lake Superior Museum of Transportation, a Depot member agency. Courtesy, Duluth Convention and Visitors Bureau*

for significantly undercounting its residents. A controversial five-year school consolidation plan was adopted by the Duluth School Board in late 1981. That plan called for the closing of as many as 10 elementary schools, four of six junior high schools, and one of four senior highs. (UMD, however, continued its steady growth, in 1981 posting an enrollment of more than 7,500.)

Yet Duluth has not surrendered its pride or its plans for a better future. Industrial and business development efforts, which have for years been carried on with praiseworthy albeit small-scale success by the port authority and the city itself, have found new and active allies in business, in labor, indeed in all segments of the community. In March 1982 the editors of the *News-Tribune,* the journalistic heirs of Thomas Preston Foster who 114 years earlier had sung the coming glories of the Zenith City of the Unsalted Seas, endorsed a booster campaign—"We're Duluth. And proud of it!"—of which Foster might well have been proud.

The depressed state of the national economy sometimes seems more exaggerated here—in some ways it is—leaving many in the area pessimistic about the future. Still, most of us are proud of our city, and there's every reason to be confident that things will get better.

Duluth today remains a proud community. Its citizens are proud of their history and heritage and look with pride and confidence to their future. Duluthians strongly identify not only with their city, but often also with the neighborhoods in which they live; be it Piedmont Heights or Park Point, Lakeside or Fond du Lac, community clubs and neighborhood organizations are active in civic and social affairs ranging from youth sports to school councils to garden clubs to home rehabilitation to housing projects for the elderly.

Ethnic roots also are strong in the Zenith City's community life. Since the summer day in 1869 when pioneer Duluthians took time from their city-building chores to welcome a boatload of some 200 Swedish immigrants to town, Duluth's population has been a smorgasbord of nationalities. The early waves of migration to Duluth and the Head of the Lakes region brought mainly northern Europeans—Swedes, Norwegians, Finns and Germans. (To this day, both the Swedish and Finnish governments maintain consular offices in Duluth.) They were followed later by tides of Poles, Italians, Irishmen, Scotsmen, Russians, and delegations from most other corners of the world.

These immigrants often settled with other of their countrymen in ethnic enclaves in the city's sundry neighborhoods. Their cultural celebrations became noteworthy social events for the entire community—for decades, the Swedish Midsummer Festival in Lincoln Park was one of the biggest events of the year for all Duluthians. The immigrants also formed fraternal lodges and self-help societies and erected halls, churches, and synagogues to foster and preserve the heritage of their native lands. Many of these edifices still serve the social, educational, and religious needs of the children and grandchildren of their founders.

And the descendents of these early Duluthians continue to proudly parade their origins during the annual Duluth Folk Festival. The event is held the first weekend in August in Leif Erikson Park. There, dozens of nationalities gather to entertain each other with their distinctive music and folk dances and to sample for a day the foods brought here by their forefathers.

Another ethnic footnote in Duluth's history was recorded in 1982 with the sailing of the vessel *Hjemkomst* (Norwegian for "homecoming"). The 76-foot wooden craft, a replica of those sailed by the Vikings 10 centuries ago, was painstakingly constructed by Robert Asp, a schoolteacher from Hawley, Minnesota, who intended to sail it from Duluth to his parents' native home of Norway, retracing the route of the ancient Vikings and that of the

42-foot *Leif Erikson* which sailed into Duluth in 1927. Although Asp died before realizing his dream, his children carried on their father's quest. On a blustery May day, thousands of Duluthians turned out to wish a safe and speedy voyage to the *Hjemkomst* and her crew as they sailed beneath the Aerial Bridge. The tiny ship and its crew of 11 reached Bergen, Norway on July 17.

Duluth's self-pride is evident to citizens and tourists alike as they tour the city. Well-kept parks and public playgrounds are scattered along tree-lined streets and boulevards. Attractive homes, from modest to stately, sit along many of these thoroughfares. And a consortium of historically and aesthetically concerned citizens, the Duluth Preservation Alliance, has for several years been working diligently to preserve the city's architectural heritage. Alliance members have restored many of Duluth's older homes to their grand appearances during the city's most prosperous days.

Tourism is one of Duluth's brightest hopes for the future. (Among others are the city's role as a regional education center— UMD has been one of the few college campuses in Minnesota to show consistent enrollment increases—and as a regional health care center.) Annually, hundreds of thousands of people come to Duluth for conventions and to enjoy the city's scenic attractions.

These include, in addition to a drive along the Skyline Parkway with its vistas of Lake Superior and of the Twin Ports harbor's panoply of world commerce: excursion boat tours of that harbor; the Depot, which truly is a stunning repository for the region's history and heritage; the Canal Park Marine Museum, with its praiseworthy collection of Great Lakes maritime memorabilia; and Glensheen, the turn-of-the-century lakeshore mansion of timber and mineral baron Chester Congdon now operated as a museum and conference center by UMD. Thousands of other tourists annually stop off in Duluth en route to the wilderness regions of far northern Minnesota and Ontario.

Winter tourism and cold-weather activities have also been steadily growing, this despite Mark Twain's oft-cited (at least in Duluth) avowal: "The coldest winter I ever spent was a summer in Duluth." Duluthians take an almost vain pride in the length and harshness of the winter season, and annually more and more people from other regions are joining them for the experience. Downhill skiing at Spirit Mountain is a popular pastime, and cross-country skiing is gathering a large following. Duluth remains a training ground for some of the United States' top ski jumpers. Ice fishing is a sport practiced by many, and ice skating is an avocation for nearly all young Duluthians; UMD annually fields one of the best collegiate hocky teams in the nation.

While some may proclaim that the Zenith City never has attained Thomas Preston Foster's visionary metropolitan status as "a great city . . . the abode of commerce and manufactures and refinement and civilization," Duluth has carved a niche for itself in the American scene. It is a place which Duluthians occupy with pride and which many of them labor daily to promulgate for themselves and for their children.

Skyline reflections in the sparkling bay emphasize the beauty of Duluth's natural setting. Photo by Wayne Gatlin

Eastman Johnson painted Notin e Garbowik, or "Lady Standing with the Wind," in 1857 while visiting his sister Sara in Superior, Wisconsin. Richard Teller Crane purchased Johnson's collection of Indian artwork for Duluth following the artist's death in 1906. The collection is on permanent display at the St. Louis County Historical Society.

The library's "Minnehaha" stained glass window, designed by Duluthian Anne Vanderlipp Weston, was made in the New York studios of Louis C. Tiffany. In 1893, area women donated the window to the public library and now it hangs in the St. Louis County Heritage and Arts Center. Courtesy, Duluth Public Library

Left: *A blue robe of woolen cloth, held by red shoulder straps similar to that worn by the Chippewa woman in this 1857 Eastman Johnson painting is on display at the St. Louis County Historical Society exhibit at the Depot. Photo by Bruce Ojard*

Below: *The original picture,* Double Head Study—Indians, *now part of the St. Louis County Historical Society's collection, was painted by noted portrait artist, Eastman Johnson, during a visit to Duluth-Superior in 1857. Photo by Bruce Ojard*

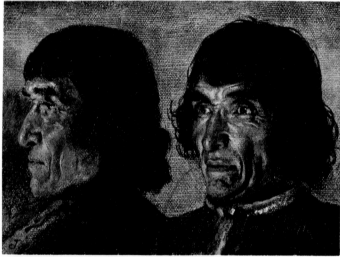

Left: *This tikinagan or cradle board displays the artistic beadwork skills of the Anishinabe or Chippewa people. It is part of the native American Indian culture exhibit in the Sieur du Lhut Room of the St. Louis County Historical Society in the Depot. Photo by Bruce Ojard*

Left: *Another of Eastman Johnson's paintings features two Chippewa women in their native dress. The painting is part of the collection on display at the St. Louis County Historical Society.*

Left: *The first ore train of the Duluth and Iron Range Railroad heads for Two Harbors from Soudan on July 31, 1884 in this watercolor by Howard Fogg. From King,* The Missabe Road, *1972*

Left: *The last of the Minnesota ore-hauling mallet trains of the Duluth, Missabe and Iron Range Railway heads for Two Harbors in this watercolor by Howard Fogg. From King,* The Missabe Road, *1972*

HE SUBSTITUTES FOR US
LET US SUBSTITUTE FOR HIM

M.314, FOOD CONSERVATION DEPT. PUBLIC LIBRA

CONTENTS 12 FL. OZ.

Fitger's

PREMIUM PALE BEER

FITGER BREWING COMPANY, DULUTH, MINN.

INTERNAL REVENUE TAX PAID

PERFECTOS

CLASS

COL. CLARO

STONE-ORDEAN-WELLS

HONEYCOMB

Clas

Left: *The Romanesque-style Central High School designed by Duluth architects Palmer and Hall has dominated the skyline from Second Street and Lake Avenue since 1892. Since the construction of a new High School on Central Entrance in 1971, the massive sandstone school has served as the Central Administration Building for the Duluth schools. Photo by Wayne Gatlin*

Below: *Cascade Park lies on a steep hill at the top of First Avenue West. Obtained by the city in 1869, it featured elaborate masonry and a waterfall formed by Clark House Creek. The ornate bell tower blew down in 1897 but was reconstructed with Model City funds in 1975. Courtesy, Duluth Public Library*

Above: *The chateau-like Union Depot, created by Boston architects Peabody and Stearns in 1890, reminds Duluth of its French influence. Placed on the National Register of Historic Places in 1971, it is now Duluth's cultural center, the St. Louis County Heritage and Arts Center. Photo by Wayne Gatlin*

Right: *One of Duluth's earliest gas filling-stations, Northwestern Oil Company, began in 1921. Located on East Superior Street, the building survived, and is now the October House, a women's clothing store. Courtesy, Duluth Public Library*

Top: *A view of downtown Duluth features architectural landmarks, modern offices, hotels and a retail complex. Photo by Wayne Gatlin*

A modern building at Fifth Avenue West and First Street houses the Herald and News-Tribune, *Duluth's and the northland's newspaper for more than 100 years. Courtesy, Duluth Public Library*

The Canal Park Marine Museum next to the Aerial Lift Bridge on Lake Avenue is operated by the Army Corps of Engineers. Courtesy, Duluth Public Library

Below: *The William Prin-*
dle home is typical of the
ornate homes built during
Duluth's 1890-1900
building spree. The three-
story grey stucco was
designed by William A.
Hunt in 1905. Courtesy,
Duluth Public Library

Right: *Mining executive*
Joseph Sellwood gave this
home to his daughter
Othelia when she married
L.W. Leithead. Similar to
a sandstone fortress, it was
designed by Palmer, Hall,
and Hunt in 1902. Cour-
tesy, Duluth Public Library

Left: *John and Betsy*
Brandin's home at 1114
East Second Street was
built in 1892. The house
was recently restored and
converted into a duplex by
Laurel Ulland of the
Ulland Restoration Project.
Courtesy, Laurel Ulland

Above: *Frederic W. Paine*
commissioned architect
Bertram Goodhue to
design this English Stone
barn on his "Sunrise Ter-
race" farm near Amity
Creek. Courtesy, Duluth
Public Library

This sturdy yellow brick home on London Road was designed by W.T. Bray about 1910 for Newell F. Russell, a partner in the Bridgeman Russell Creamery. Courtesy, Duluth Public Library

This remodeled carriage house on the Washburn property at the end of Butte Street was for many years a summer home for Genevieve Washburn, daughter of Duluth attorney and business leader, Jed L. Washburn. Courtesy, Duluth Public Library

Above: *A parade of nations opened the annual Folk Festival in August 1977 in Leif Erikson Park, located on the shoreline of Lake Superior at 12th Avenue East. Courtesy, Duluth Public Library*

Right: *World-wide curling teams compete at the Silver Broom Competition in 1976 at the Duluth Arena. Curling has been a popular sport in Duluth since Christmas Day, 1891 when the Duluth Curling Club played its first game. Courtesy, Duluth Public Library*

Right: *Skiers enjoy Duluth's spectacular scenery on the chairlift at Spirit Mountain. The ski area has 14 slopes for downhill skiers and 17.5 kilometers of cross-country trails. Photo by Wayne Gatlin*

Top: *A brisk breeze moves a group of sailboats along Duluth's shoreline, adding grace to the choppy waters of Lake Superior. Photo by Wayne Gatlin*

Above: *Battling ice, a tug works in the harbor at the end of shipping season. Photo by Wayne Gatlin*

Left: *Ice fishing is one of the many winter recreational opportunities in Duluth, for those brave enough to face freezing temperatures on the frozen lake. Courtesy, Duluth Public Library*

The shoreline of Lake Superior, the world's largest body of fresh water, can be seen from Duluth's London Road that leads to the North Shore Drive and Canada. Photo by Wayne Gatlin

The granite sphinxes in front of architect Thomas A. Vecchi's residence on London Road were placed there by an earlier tenant who purchased them from the Greene Olsen Memorials Inc. in the early 1960s. Vecchi's 1890 home was built by the Lakeside Land Company that developed the London Road Addition. Courtesy, Duluth Public Library

Early loggers boomed and towed logs down the St. Louis River, through what is now Jay Cooke State Park. Courtesy, Duluth Public Library

The walleye, Minnesota's official state fish, inhabits the shallows of Lake Superior and most Minnesota lakes. The walleye is a favorite of Minnesota fishermen. Photo by Wayne Gatlin

The city-owned Duluth Arena-Auditorium sits astride Superior Bay overlooking the port's diverse maritime commerce. The most prominent and successful undertaking of the city's 1960s urban renewal programs, it is now the Zenith City's convention and cultural center, hosting such diverse activities as curling, rodeos, rock concerts, high school and collegiate hockey, and the Duluth-Superior Symphony Orchestra. Photo by Wayne Gatlin

A wide-angle view of the Duluth-Superior Harbor features Park Point and the Aerial Lift Bridge in the foreground. The city of Superior can be seen in background. Photo by Wayne Gatlin

*Memories of Duluth
always include golden
sunrises over the lake.
Photo by Wayne Gatlin*

*Ore boats such as the
Thomas W. Lamont are
common sights at Duluth's
docks. Photo by Wayne
Gatlin*

*The Aerial Lift Bridge
frames the Arena-Audito-
rium, Duluth's convention
and entertainment center.
Photo by Wayne Gatlin*

*When night turns the city lights along the terraced hills into a diamond crown and the moon hangs over the silver
bridge, Duluth has a magical charm. Photo by Bruce Ojard*

Chapter Seven

PARTNERS IN PROGRESS

By William Beck

Duluth always has been a logical place for trade. In the beginning, French, British, and American traders established fur posts at the Head of the Lakes. Next came commercial fishermen, casting their nets along the North Shore of Lake Superior and reaping the bounty of the deepest, largest, and coldest of the Great Lakes. The opening of the bonanza farms in the Red River Valley of Minnesota and North Dakota resulted in the construction of terminal elevators at Duluth and neighboring Superior, Wisconsin. Over the past century a veritable flood of grain has flowed through the Twin Ports down the lakes to feed America and the world.

The discovery of literally mountains of soft, red iron ore on northern Minnesota's Vermilion, Mesabi, and Cuyuna iron ranges made Duluth the busiest bulk-commodity port in America in the early years of the 20th century. The railroad lines that ended at Rice's Point also were the land terminus for millions of board feet of pine and hardwood from the almost limitless forests stretching north and east from Duluth.

The depletion of the rich iron ore resources by the nation's defense needs during World War II caused some pessimists to predict the demise of the local economy. But the development of taconite—a low-grade, flint-hard iron ore that is processed into marble-size pellets—rejuvenated the Mesabi Range and the iron ports of Lake Superior. The discovery of immense low-sulfur coal deposits in Montana and Wyoming led to the development of coal transshipment facilities at the Head of the Lakes. Low-sulfur coal is expected to be shipped from the Twin Ports in ever-increasing tonnages as the federal government requires electric utilities and industries in the Great Lakes states to reduce the amount of sulfur burned in coal-fired plants.

Entrepreneurs and venture capitalists took advantage of Duluth's position as one of the nation's premiere shipping locations. The city nestled between the rock bluffs and Lake Superior spawned a host of industries catering to maritime and transportation interests. Shipbuilding has been an integral part of Duluth since its earliest days. Bulk ore carriers and lumber packets were built there before the turn of the century, and both world wars saw frenetic activity in the shipyards of the Twin Ports. During World War II alone, some 300 vessels were built in Duluth and Superior for the Allied war effort, including Coast Guard cutters that are still in service today.

The slowdown in taconite and wood processing since 1980 is once again raising the specter of the city's industrial future. But Duluth has rebounded from adversity before: It came back early in the century when lumber shipments through the port dried up almost overnight; it came back after iron ore shipments nearly disappeared in the 1950s; it came back when shipments of coal up the Great Lakes were replaced by low-sulfur Montana coal moving down the lakes; and it will come back from the recession of the early 1980s.

On the following pages you will meet many of the organizations that are an integral part of Duluth's resilient and industrious business community.

ST. LOUIS COUNTY HISTORICAL SOCIETY

To people in Duluth, it's known simply as the Depot. Located at Fifth Avenue West and Michigan Street, the Chateauesque Style structure houses the St. Louis County Historical Society. When it was designed 90 years ago by Boston architects Robert Swain Peabody and John Goddard Stearns, the building was known as the Duluth Union Depot, and it served as the railroad passenger terminus for travelers in the Twin Ports area. The East Coast architects were no strangers to working in the Midwest; they came to Duluth from St. Paul, where they had been commissioned to design the Summit Avenue mansion of Great Northern Railroad magnate James J. Hill.

In 1977 the St. Louis County Historical Society moved into the Depot, which by then had officially been renamed the St. Louis County Heritage and Arts Center. Part of an innovative program combining the area's history with cultural activities, the Depot houses the Duluth-Superior Symphony Orchestra, the Duluth Art Institute, Duluth Playhouse, Matinee Musicale, and Duluth Ballet. The collections of the St. Louis County Historical Society Museum—including exhibits depicting early exploration, the native American history of the region, the fur trade, and life on the logging frontier—share space with the A.M. Chisholm Museum and the Lake Superior Museum of Transportation.

Located on the lower track level of the Depot, the Lake Superior Museum of Transportation is a collection of railroad history and memorabilia unparalleled in the Upper Midwest. Among the exhibits are the 1861 *William Crooks,* the first locomotive to run in Minnesota; the 1870 wood-burning *Minnetonka;* and one of the giant Mallet steam engines that hauled train loads of iron ore from the nearby Mesabi Range to the ore docks in Duluth.

In June 1982 the Depot Square exhibit opened. It includes 20 storefronts bordering the trackage of the Lake Superior Museum of Transportation, which recreates a typical Duluth street at the beginning of the 20th century.

The 20th century was a little over two decades old when the St. Louis County Historical Society was established in 1922 by a group of Duluth citizens led by William E. Culkin. Lawrence J. Sommer, director of the Society since 1977, said St. Louis county was one of the first counties in the state to organize a historical society. Although the State Historical Society dates back to the territorial period in the middle of the 19th century, most county historical societies in the state of Minnesota were not established until the 1950s and 1960s.

In its earliest years, the Society was tucked away in a corner of the county courthouse in Duluth, moving in 1943 to a room in Tweed Hall on the campus of the old Duluth State Teacher's College. Four years later the Society moved its collection to the George Stone Mansion at 2228 East Superior Street, which was home for the organization until it moved to the Depot in 1977. That same year the Society joined with the University of Minnesota-Duluth and the Minnesota Historical Society to establish the northeast Minnesota Historical Center, a regional archives and manuscript collection located on the campus of UMD. It is the largest collection of its kind in the state outside the Twin Cities metropolitan area.

The St. Louis County Historical Society on West Michigan Street. (Photo courtesy of Bruce Ojard.)

———

Various antiques can be seen at the Society's headquarters. (Photo courtesy of Bruce Ojard.)

FIRST BANK-DULUTH

The new century was in its infancy in 1902, and the port of Duluth was bustling with activity from lake shipments of the rich red iron ore of the Mesabi Range, opened less than a decade before. The

In 1910 Northern National Bank, a forerunner of First Bank-Duluth, moved into Minnesota's tallest structure—the newly completed 16-story Alworth Building.

———

booming business climate required new sources of capital, prompting the founding of the Duluth Savings Bank in offices upstairs in the old Herald Building of West Superior Street and the City National Bank that year.

The Duluth Savings Bank secured a national bank charter in 1909 and changed its name to the Northern National Bank. The next May the newly renamed bank moved into new quarters on West Superior Street, in the recently completed 16-story Alworth Building, Duluth's first skyscraper.

The third of the three banks that would later merge to form one of Duluth's largest financial institutions was founded in 1920 as the Minnesota National Bank. The three banks weathered the slow years of the Depression in Duluth and bounced back strongly with the wartime economy of the

early 1940s.

Then, in June 1947, Northern National consolidated with Minnesota National to form the Northern Minnesota National Bank, at the time the second-largest independently owned bank in the Ninth Federal Reserve District. With resources and assets of almost $44 million—more than 40 times the assets and resources of the predecessor

Duluth Savings Bank when it began 45 years before—the newly consolidated bank moved in 1948 into new quarters at 306 West Superior. The four-story building that became the headquarters of Northern Minnesota National was later expanded in 1959 and was solidly constructed, using materials like Minnesota granite, Central American mahogany, and marble from Italy and Belgium.

The next major milestone came in the fall of 1957 with the merger of Northern Minnesota National Bank and City National Bank. City National in its early years had been located down the street from Duluth Savings Bank at 314 West Superior Street—today the site of the Torrey Building—and later moved to 202 West Superior, into the Sellwood Building. The consolidated bank was renamed the Northern City National Bank. With 159 employees, Northern City at the time of the merger had $71.5 million in resources, 16,000 savings accounts, and 10,000 loans of different kinds on its books, including more than 1,000 mortgages. The 1957 consolidation

also brought Northern City into affiliation with the First Bank System of St. Paul, a major Midwest multistate bank holding company.

There would be one more name change. In November 1980 Northern City National changed its name to First Bank-Duluth to reflect more closely its affiliation with the First Bank System. In January 1981, several

Construction of First Bank-Duluth's new home, First Bank Place, is under way one block east of the Alworth Building, in the heart of the downtown business district.

———

months later, First Bank-Duluth purchased the Glass Block Building—the city's major downtown department store which had closed in 1980—and announced plans to raze the old structure and build a brand-new bank headquarters on the site at Second Avenue West and Superior Street. In the summer of 1981 wrecking crews went to work on the Glass Block Building. Construction on First Bank Place began in 1983 with expected occupancy by fall of 1984.

Eighty years after two small banks began business in the Second and Third blocks west on Superior Street, First Bank-Duluth—the product of metamorphosis and change—is still doing business and is planning to be around for a long time to come.

MINNESOTA POWER

The impetus for industrial development in northern Minnesota was water power. The eastern financial interests that funded development of Minnesota's Vermilion and Mesabi iron ranges in the 1880s and 1890s needed electricity to run the machinery that separated and washed the rich red ore. The lumber barons working their way west from the white pine forests of Michigan and Wisconsin wanted to see dams on the rivers of northern Minnesota, dams that would create holding ponds for saw timber.

Minnesota Power chairman and president Jack F. Rowe at Fond du Lac Dam in 1981.

———

One of the first to notice the potential of hydropower was eastern financier Jay Cooke. Cooke never managed to see his ambitious plans to fruition, but a successor organization, the Great Northern Power Company, followed in Cooke's footsteps and built the massive Thomson Dam on the St. Louis River between 1905 and 1907. Great Northern expanded to take in several smaller utility companies during the World War I era and merged with Duluth Edison and several Cuyuna and Mesabi Range power companies to form Minnesota Power & Light Company in 1923.

All through the 1920s MP&L remained a hydro utility, but the late years of the decade brought drought to the northern Minnesota watershed. The company built a coal-fired power plant on the waterfront in

West Duluth in 1931. Later named the M.L. Hibbard steam station in honor of the longtime president of the firm, that first coal-fired plant provided much-needed construction jobs to Duluthians during the Depression.

The outbreak of World War II and the nation's incessant demand for iron snapped the Mesabi Range out of its economic doldrums almost overnight. In a crash program, additional coal-fired units were added in Duluth during the war, and a new coal-fired plant was built at Aurora-Hoyt Lakes in the early 1950s.

For a while during the 1950s, it looked as if the Mesabi Range was going to run dry, its high-grade ore resources depleted. In 1964 Minnesota voters approved an amendment to the state constitution changing the way iron ore processing companies were taxed. The change brought about the development of a taconite—a low-grade iron ore—industry on the Mesabi Range, and from the early 1960s to the mid-1970s the U.S. steel industry built eight taconite pellet plants in northeastern Minnesota, a capital investment of well over one billion dollars.

The new taconite plants spurred Minnesota Power & Light to an unprecedented amount of construction during the 1960s and 1970s. Clay Boswell, Hibbard's successor at the helm of MP&L, started the first two of four coal-fired units at Cohasset,

just west of Grand Rapids. The Cohasset units were later named in Boswell's honor, and his successors—Axel Herbert and Sylvester Laskin—expanded the plant with the addition of Unit No. Three in 1973. Under the leadership of Jack F. Rowe, who succeeded Laskin, the company spearheaded the innovative Square Butte project, completed in 1978 and consisting of a new lignite-fired power plant in western North Dakota linked to northern Minnesota by a

Construction of the dam at Fond du Lac on the St. Louis River during the 1920s.

———

high-voltage, direct-current transmission line. The crown jewel of the Minnesota Power system, the 500-megawatt Boswell Unit No. Four, followed and came onstream in 1980.

Today Minnesota Power—the company shortened its name in 1981 to reflect its traditional role as an energy supplier and its intent to investigate diversification possibilities—serves a 26,000-square-mile area of northern Minnesota. Its 1,400 employees are part of a $400-million annual enterprise, and its power plants burn close to four million tons of Montana coal each year. It continues to provide reliable electric energy to its residential, commercial, and industrial customers and looks forward confidently to the challenges posed through the rest of the century.

DULUTH, WINNIPEG & PACIFIC RAILROAD

The majestic stands of white pine stretching across entire counties in northeastern Minnesota attracted loggers and railroad men to the Lake Superior arrowhead country in the years just before and after the turn of the century.

Wirt Cook and William O'Brien amassed substantial pine holdings in the 1890s just west of Virginia, and in the summer of 1901 the two men built the Duluth, Virginia and Rainy Lake Railway to connect their holdings with sawmills at Silver Lake. During the next two years the infant railroad added trackage north to Cook, 65 miles from the Canadian border at International Falls-Fort Frances. North of the border, the Mackenzie-Mann interests were extending their Canadian Northern Railroad from Winnipeg to Fort Frances. In 1905 the Canadian Northern purchased the Duluth, Virginia and Rainy Lake, rechristened it the Duluth, Rainy Lake and Winnipeg Railway Company, and began construction to close the rail gap between Cook and the border.

The connection was completed in the spring of 1908, and just one year later the Canadians incorporated the Duluth, Winnipeg and Pacific Railroad to build 81 miles

of track from just north of Virginia to the Twin Ports of Duluth-Superior. It took three years for the completion of the final link between the Canadian border and Duluth, including blasting the only railroad tunnel in Minnesota and four miles of rail right-of-way through solid granite. The road dropped 800 feet in the last few miles leading to the DW&P's West Duluth Depot.

This photo taken in the 1950s reflects a DW&P's busy West Duluth yard facility.

LCL (less than carload) rail shipments were received at Duluth, Winnipeg & Pacific's West Duluth freight office until the mid-1940s.

The parent Canadian Northern was absorbed into the Canadian National system just after World War I. South of the border, the Duluth, Winnipeg and Pacific had an exclusive contract to haul the output of the massive Virginia and Rainy Lake Mill, estimated at 200 million saw logs a year. The DW&P had its own lumber dock in Duluth, in addition to hauling lumber into the Twin Ports for rail transfer south.

The white pine timber industry declined after the Great Depression, steam-generated locomotion ended in 1956 with the advent of diesel power, and the last passenger service ran in 1961. The Duluth, Winnipeg and Pacific, however, continues as one of the major overland bridge routes linking the United States and Canada. The 167 miles of main rail line extending from the border at Ranier, Minnesota, to the yard in Duluth connect the CN Rail system with six U.S. carriers hauling potash, lumber, wood pulp, and paper as its chief commodities.

In 1971 CN Rail formed the Grand Trunk Corporation. The DW&P, now part of that corporation, plans to relocate its Duluth facilities to nearby Superior because of the construction of Interstate 35 through Duluth—readying the railroad for service to northeastern Minnesota in the 21st century.

ST. MARY'S HOSPITAL

In the early days of the white pine timber industry in northern Minnesota, an accident in the woods often meant disaster for the affected lumberjack. Even if he could get to a hospital in time, the "jack" was faced with the problem of paying for his stay in those days before medical insurance.

That is, unless he had the foresight to purchase a lumberjack hospital ticket from Sister Amata of St. Mary's Hospital in Duluth. Costing 75 cents per month, the hospital ticket entitled the purchaser to medical care and a bed in the hospital, which opened early in 1888 at 20th Avenue West and Third Street. The innovative medical insurance plan, one of the first of its kind in the nation, was a hallmark of the order of Benedictine Sisters who opened a convent in Duluth in the mid-1880s from their motherhouse near St. Cloud.

In those early days, years ending in "eight" seemed to portend momentous things for the Duluth hospital. St. Mary's opened its doors in 1888 and in 1898 moved a little over three miles east to its present site at Fifth Avenue East and Third Street. In 1918 the hospital's staff was tested by a terrible outbreak of Spanish influenza and by an October forest fire in Carlton and St. Louis counties that sent hundreds of victims to Duluth hospitals. In both cases, the St. Mary's staff came through with flying colors.

The story of St. Mary's has been primarily a story of growth. A first addition to the Fifth Avenue East site was built in 1911, and an X-ray department was added the following year — just in time to provide jobs for the first graduating class of the St. Mary's School of Nursing. The sisters went back to the bricks and mortar once again in 1922, overseeing construction of a six-story addition that effectively doubled the number of patients St. Mary's could serve. The new wing was the hospital's response to the first postwar baby boom of this century, containing delivery rooms, a nursery, and a pediatrics department.

Expansion was again the watchword during the 1950s. A psychiatric unit was constructed in 1955, and a nine-story wing to the hospital was completed in 1957. The additional 131-bed capacity of the new wing

St. Mary's Hospital provided modern health care to the growing region of northeastern Minnesota and northwestern Wisconsin in 1928. The old east wing (pictured on the right) was replaced by a more modern facility in 1969.

allowed much-needed remodeling in other areas of the hospital and left room for dedicating an entire floor to a surgical suite.

Today St. Mary's has reached the brink of yet another expansion, which has created a cardiac surgery unit and a new newborn intensive care unit. Now licensed for 380 beds and staffed by 1,500 employees, St. Mary's continues to provide comprehensive health care for the people of northeastern Minnesota and northwestern Wisconsin — much as it did when Sister Amata and six fellow Benedictine Sisters looked after the physical well-being of the north woods lumberjacks.

With over 1,500 skilled employees, St. Mary's continues to grow as a regional medical center.

REACH-ALL MANUFACTURING AND ENGINEERING INC.

Jim Raymond's first aerial device — built specifically to assist his own tree-trimming work in 1961.

Reach-All Manufacturing and Engineering Inc. was conceived as the inventive response to the problems encountered in another business. When Jim Raymond started Arrowhead Tree Service in the early 1950s, several of his early contracts involved brush clearing for electric utilities in the bogs and forests of northeastern Minnesota and northwestern Wisconsin. A traveling foreman for the American Tree Company, Raymond had been transferred to Duluth from Deerwood, Minnesota, in 1949 and had stayed on to found his own tree service in the Twin Ports.

Since much of the work a tree service performs is literally up in the air, Raymond tinkered with designs of equipment that would make the job easier. In 1964 Arrowhead Tree Service partners Raymond and Bill Sazma incorporated Reach-All to manufacture truck-mounted telescoping booms with an attached man-basket at the end. It was, quite simply, an idea whose time had come.

Two years after opening a manufacturing facility at 436 Calvary Road, Reach-All had already built 50 pieces of equipment. That spring of 1966, the firm constructed six of the aerial baskets for the North Dakota

Highway Department, and orders began coming in from electric utilities, telephone companies, sign firms, and contractors. The largest unit built at the plant was capable of placing a man 70 feet in the air.

By the mid-1970s Reach-All was operating out of a 22,500-square-foot metal building and several smaller facilities clustered at the Calvary Road site. The company was constructing units able to lift a man up to 125 feet, and it had secured an order for 376 cranes from the Penn Central Railroad, the largest order in its history.

Reach-All also has become more heavily involved with the export market as it has gained expertise in marketing its products. The firm built a special unit mounted on a Bombardier snow track for work in the Beaufort Sea oil fields of Alaska's North Slope, and in 1978 it shipped four units to

Aramco in Saudi Arabia. The 125-foot units were mounted on trucks equipped with special balloon tires and were used to erect high transmission electric lines in the desert oil fields.

As the 1980s began Reach-All was selling 30 percent of its product line overseas. But the firm has never forgotten its Duluth roots. In 1982 Reach-All's 150 employees required an annual payroll of two million dollars, and the firm pledged to assist the local economy by increasing its purchase of supplies in the Duluth area.

———

The 1982 Reach-All model HD5150—an aerial device with a 150-foot working height—is one of a variety of Reach-Alls which range in working height from 33 to 170 feet.

CLYDE IRON

Building the equipment used to extract natural resources from the earth has been the stock-in-trade of Duluth's "Clyde" facilities for over 80 years.

Founded in 1899 as the Northwestern Manufacturing Company, the firm originally produced the stamp hammers the lumberjacks in the nearby pine woods of Minnesota, Wisconsin, and Michigan used to brand cut logs. The city of Duluth then had only half the population it has now, but it was the headquarters for a major white pine timber industry. Duluth sawmills cut some 440 million board feet of lumber in 1902.

Just the year before, the nine employees of Northwestern Manufacturing started producing a steam log jammer, or loader. It had been developed at the turn of the century by John R. McGiffert, a Duluth

This barge-mounted Whirley, built by Clyde, has a 2,000-pound lifting capacity, with modifications available to lift 3,000 pounds. Clyde has just furnished another crane of the same capacity, completing testing in February 1983. The barge can house up to 550 people and is used worldwide for offshore oil exploration construction.

attorney with goals to make a mark in history through inventions. Mounted on a railroad car with a swinging boom, the McGiffert log loader and its companion jammer, the Decker log loader, soon were familiar sights in logging districts all over the world.

After the disappearance of horses from

Mounted on a railroad car with a swinging boom, these traveling log unloaders were a familiar sight in the logging areas of northern Minnesota, Wisconsin, and Michigan around 1910.

the woods following World War I, the business was renamed "Clyde Iron." It continued to make logging equipment, coming up with a gasoline log skidder and a skidder attachment for the then-popular Fordson tractor. The company also made handling equipment for sugar cane growers.

As the 1920s progressed, the firm's plant at 29th Avenue West and Michigan Street turned more and more to the construction of hoists and derricks. Clyde engineers were in the forefront of designing what was then sophisticated hoisting technology, and the company's advertising slogan during the 1930s was "You'll take pride in your Clyde."

The development of specialized logging trucks and the onset of the Great Depression spelled the end of an era for steam log loaders. But Clyde diversified more heavily into hoisting equipment, securing a license just before World War II from the Wiley Crane Company of Port Deposit, Maryland, for the manufacture of the Whirley crane.

The organization's engineers redesigned

the Wiley Whirley for shipyard use, making possible, just in time for World War II, a new method of large ship construction. Clyde was no stranger to defense work; during World War I the firm had built numerous hoists and derricks for use by the American Expeditionary Force in France. But Clyde's workers took to defense work with a vengeance from 1942 to 1945.

American shipbuilders used the Whirleys built by Clyde Iron to assemble the merchantmen and fighting ships that helped win the war for the Allies. The work started at home. Shipbuilders in the Port of Duluth won $34 million in contracts during 1941 alone; before the war was over, 355 ships were built at the Head of Lake Superior for the war effort. Clyde-built cranes, hoists, and derricks went with American fighting men around the world, helping to unload ships wherever port facilities were limited or nonexistent, keeping the lines of supplies open for the combat forces. In the spring of 1945, when American armies were poised on the west bank of the Rhine River for the final thrust into Nazi Germany, a Clyde rig helped throw the first Allied bridge across the Rhine, the last German defense line.

Clyde Iron's contribution to the American war effort did not go unrecognized. On October 7, 1942, U.S. Navy Captain Sam Colby Lewis, Chicago, presented the Army/Navy "E" Award to Clyde president C.A. Luster and vice-president J.R. McGiffert. The big red and blue "E" pennant was awarded at a ceremony in Duluth, which was attended by the plant's more than 400 workers and some 600 guests. The pennant was given to Clyde in recognition of the firm's engineering efficiency and machine production; before hostilities ceased in 1945, Clyde was allowed to add four production stars to the coveted pennant.

Following the war Clyde continued as a leader in its field, designing and producing sophisticated revolving cranes. By 1955 the company had the capacity of manufacturing a Whirley crane every month. Its Whirleys were used in the construction of dams, nuclear power stations, buildings, and bridges. In 1961 Clyde Iron constructed the world's largest portable hoist for a New York contractor working on the Brooklyn Narrows Bridge. The hoist measured 39 feet long with a line pull of 42,000 pounds. American Bridge Corporation used Clyde equipment in the construction of the "Mighty Mac," the bridge spanning the Straits of Mackinac between Michigan's Upper and Lower Peninsula. Clyde also built two 90-ton gantry mounted cranes for its home port of Duluth in 1959 along with many other ports throughout the world. Today Clyde builds hoists up to 300,000 pounds line pull.

A major new application for Clyde products came in 1965, when the Duluth firm built a 500-ton Whirley crane for an offshore oil rig in the Gulf of Mexico off Louisiana. The largest in the world to that time, the boom was 245 feet long, and the 500-ton lift was equivalent to taking 250 automobiles and putting them on top of a 17-story building. That year, the 500-ton Whirley was recognized by the Minnesota Society of Professional Engineers as one of the Seven Engineering Wonders of Minnesota.

To date Clyde has built more than twice as many 500-ton and over capacity cranes as all the rest of the crane manufacturers in the world combined. In the 1970s Clyde built even bigger cranes—a 1,600-ton barge-mounted Whirley in 1973 (for which it won its second Engineering Wonders award) and seven 2,000-ton cranes. Clyde's

In 1926, as Clyde Iron Works was progressing from logging equipment to hoists and derricks, the employees posed for this photo.

————

Duluth plant—modernized in a $3-million expansion in 1974—has also built two 2,400-ton cranes, and a crane in the 3,500-ton range is now in the design stage. They also supplement their work force by building hoists and anchor winches for all types of applications throughout the world.

As Clyde Iron (presently known only as Clyde) nears its century mark in Duluth, it continues its business of building the equipment that allows man to hoist and lift the fruits of his labors.

————

Clyde Whirleys, such as this 1,600-ton capacity ship-mounted model, are used by companies worldwide for heavy offshore lifting.

ZENITH DREDGE COMPANY

Moving the bulk commodities of Minnesota and the Dakotas down the Great Lakes requires a substantial amount of maintenance and dredging of the channels, slips, and harbors.

Zenith Dredge Company was incorporated in March 1905 with the purchase of a dipper dredge and three dump scows from James Pryor, a Houghton, Michigan, businessman. The incorporators—Robert B. Whiteside, Daniel D. Murray, and Alexander S. McDonald (all from northern Minnesota)—found a location for their new company the next year and purchased land in Duluth at the foot of 13th Avenue West and the waterfront. The business expanded quickly during the next several years. In 1907 Zenith purchased additional equipment from Pryor, including another dipper dredge, more scows, and two tugboats. An 18-inch hydraulic dredge was added to the fleet in 1911.

Donald B. MacDonald started his family's long involvement with Zenith when he became a director in 1912. Two years later

The Zenith Dredge Company headquarters is located at 200 South Central Avenue, Duluth.

MacDonald was elevated to the presidency of the firm, a position he would hold until 1935, and one that his son, Donald C. MacDonald would hold from 1942 until 1972. He was then elected to the office of chairman of the board and Howard T. Hagen was elected to succeed him as president. Both continue to serve as officers and directors.

During the 1930s Zenith bought, filled, and sold numerous parcels of waterfront property including the present-day sites of Superwood Corporation, the Hibbard Steam Electric Generating Plant of Minnesota Power, a part of Hallet Dock No. Five, and several of the grain terminal elevators

The Zenith Dredge Company tug Essayons *was a familiar sight on the Duluth waterfront.*

in the Duluth-Superior Harbor. Until the late 1930s the dredging business was very steady as the Great Lakes harbors were deepened to cope with the expanding capacity of the iron ore fleet. The foresight of the navigation interests paid off handsomely during World War II, when iron ore from Minnesota literally flowed down the lakes to the mills and factories of the industrial heartland. In 1942 alone, 92 million tons of ore passed through the Great Lakes ports.

Besides having played a part in the harbor-deepening programs, Zenith aided the war effort in another way. In 1941 and 1942 contracts were secured for the construction of 10 Cactus Class Coast Guard cutters. Before the war was over Zenith built 17 cutters for the U.S. Coast Guard and 10 tankers and three net layers for the U.S. Navy. The company joined several other Duluth-Superior shipyards and manufacturing firms in receiving the Army/Navy "E" award for exceptional industrial effort.

Diversification was the order of the day in the postwar years. Although the firm won major contracts to build the breakwater at

Two Harbors for the Army Corps of Engineers in the late 1940s and the site development for the Seaway Port Authority of Duluth in the 1950s, Zenith branched out into Superwood Corporation and other ventures. Diversified subsidiaries included Arrowhead Blacktop Company, Zenith Concrete Products Company, and Zenith Terrace Mobile Home Park.

A stone quarry operation for the breakwater construction field led to the expansion into bituminous paving contracting, specializing in the surfacing of city streets and county and state highways. Concrete products manufacturing, although started in Duluth, was later transferred to Osseo, Minnesota. Construction of the mobile home park was started in 1967 and ultimately housed 290 tenants when it was sold to a private group in 1981.

Zenith has been deeply involved in specialized areas of construction and industrial development for over three-quarters of a century.

SUPERWOOD CORPORATION

The war in Europe had been over for just a few days when Donald C. MacDonald, president of Zenith Dredge Company, met with Lloyd K. Johnson of Duluth to incorporate the Superior Wood Products Company on May 15, 1945. Zenith had been heavily involved in defense work but as it became apparent that the Allies would win the war, in 1945 the company began to seriously consider diversification possibilities. Utilization of surplus shipyard plants and facilities for manufacturing of wood products appeared to have merit. The initial product line was developed to produce hardwood cores for furniture and desk tops, but that line was phased out in 1951. After extensive research it was determined that the manufacturing of hardboard from the fiber of local poplar trees was a relatively new process in the United States, dating from the late 1920s and early 1930s. Prior to World War II there were only three hardboard manufacturing plants in the United States, but Superior Wood Products was one of more than a dozen companies incorporated to manufacture hardboard in the immediate postwar era.

The venture, whose name was changed to Superwood Corporation in 1954, erected a pilot plant in 1948-1949 on the site of the former Zenith Shipyard at 13th Avenue West and the waterfront. The principals were joined by Morris J. Opsahl, who became president, and Kenneth V. Hafner, who became vice-president in 1954 and later succeeded Opsahl as president in 1972. MacDonald was elected to the office of chairman of the board in 1954—Johnson became senior vice-president at that time—and each of them continues to serve as an officer and director.

The 1950s and 1960s were a period of expansion for Superwood, both in Duluth and around the country. The company added three production lines—in 1952, 1956, and 1965—to its original production line at the Duluth plant. The 1956 expansion increased Superwood's working area to 140,000 square feet of space. The work force of 130 was three times the size of the crew that had manned the first production line back in the late 1940s.

Superwood acquired a hardboard plant in nearby Bemidji, Minnesota, in 1960 and in Little Rock, Arkansas, in 1961. A third plant, at Phillips, Wisconsin, was acquired in 1979. A fifth, continuous-flow process line was added at the Duluth plant in 1979.

Superwood Corporation, located at 13th Avenue West and the waterfront, is one of the major employers in the Twin Ports area. There are also Superwood plants in Bemidji, Minnesota; Phillips, Wisconsin; and Little Rock, Arkansas.

The 1970s were characterized by upheavals in several of Superwood's major markets, mainly automobiles and construction. But the firm continues to manufacture hardboard, with an annual production capacity of 600 million square feet of hardboard on a one-eighth-inch basis. In the late 1970s Superwood invested $2.5 million in wastewater treatment facilities and was one of the initial participants in the innovative plant constructed and operated by the Western Lake Superior Sanitary District. An additional $4 million was spent for pollution abatement facilities in 1982.

As Superwood enters the 1980s it remains one of the major employers in the private sector in the Twin Ports, with a work force of almost 300 at its Duluth plant and corporate headquarters. Another 350 employees are on the payroll at Superwood plants in Bemidji, Phillips, and Little Rock.

S.A. McLENNAN COMPANY

A new window to the world was opened for the Twin Ports during the first week of May 1959. Shortly after 1:15 p.m. on the third day of that month, the 457-foot *Ramon de Larrinaga* passed under the aerial bridge, the first large saltwater vessel to transit the St. Lawrence Seaway to the Head of the Lakes.

Representing the historic first "saltie" to visit Duluth was the S.A. McLennan Company vessel agency. The organization's founder, Stuart A. McLennan, a native of Duluth, began his career in the vessel business in 1937 as a vessel dispatcher employed by a local agency. The bulk cargoes of ore, taconite, coal, and grain that have been Duluth's reason for existence for more than a century require agents, brokers, and freight forwarders. After gaining 22 years of expertise in the business, and with the opportunities afforded by the opening of the Seaway, McLennan began his own enterprise in 1959.

That first year was so hectic that the fledgling agency actually was forced to turn away some business. McLennan hired Duluthian Gerald Grandmaison fresh out of college and together they worked long hours looking after crews and solving problems the vessels from around the world encountered while loading the wheat, corn, barley, and flax grown in Minnesota and the Dakotas. The salties were in port an average of eight days then—versus two days now—and McLennan was the first company in Duluth to install sophisticated communication systems to report the vessels' loading progress and prospects to offices throughout the world.

Joining the firm following his graduation from college in 1972 was McLennan's son, Mark. The S.A. McLennan Company still represents salties from around the world, but has also become the largest independent agency for domestic lake transportation in the history of Duluth. It handles as many as 1,300 shipments of grain, ore, taconite, coal, and stone annually and serves the ports of Duluth-Superior, Silver Bay, Taconite Harbor, and Ashland.

S.A. McLennan Company is one of the few Duluth vessel agencies that has been able to survive the difficulties and changes that have faced the shipping community since the opening of the Seaway 23 years ago. Stuart McLennan points out that there have been changes, both in the port and in the vessels. Sunflower seeds grown in the Red River Valley in Minnesota and North Dakota have become one of the major export cargoes out of Duluth. Very little Appalachian coal comes up the Great Lakes as in years past, but four million tons of low-sulfur Western coal goes down each year bound for electric generator plants near Detroit. Vessels have become larger and more sophisticated. In 1959 salties calling at Duluth only carried about 7,000 tons of cargo, which took about eight days to load; today they can carry up to 25,000 tons and can be loaded in as little time as 12 hours. "Lakers" in 1959 averaged about 11,000 tons of cargo; today some can carry up to 60,000 tons and can be loaded in three to four hours.

Shortly after 1:15 p.m. on May 3, 1959, the 457-foot Ramon de Larrinaga *entered Duluth harbor. It was the first saltwater vessel, or "saltie," to transit the St. Lawrence Seaway to the Head of the Lakes.*

ARROWHEAD HEARING AID CENTER

The business that one enters can sometimes be as simple a matter as asking a question and not getting an answer. That was essentially how Louise Olsen got into the retail hearing aid business in Duluth almost two decades ago.

The Alabama native was the mother of a deaf daughter who, doctors assured her, had a dead ear and couldn't be helped by the somewhat primitive hearing devices of the day. To learn more about her daughter Janet's affliction, Olsen attended courses in audiology at the Duluth campus of the University of Minnesota and still regularly attends classes and seminars.

Louise Olsen, in portrait, with her sons, Frank (left) and J.C. (right), own and operate the Arrowhead Hearing Aid Center. Mrs. Olsen became seriously involved in the audiology field because of her daughter Janet Poeschl's (center) hearing problem.

———

Shortly after taking those initial courses, Olsen, with her sons, Frank and J.C., purchased the Duluth franchise of Dahlberg Hearing Aid Company, an old-line St. Paul hearing aid manufacturer and distributor. They renamed the firm Arrowhead Hearing Aid Center in 1964, and sold and serviced hearing aids and equipment in northeastern Minnesota and neighboring northwestern Wisconsin and northern Michigan. The company's good reputation is built on dedicated, efficient, and informed good service. The office was located at Third Avenue

West and First Street, but in 1972 an optical firm expanded and Arrowhead was forced to seek another location.

The office was moved to the front of the first floor of a large brick Victorian house in East Duluth, which Olsen had purchased. It had once been home to the mining captains who were responsible for excavating the rich, red iron ore of the Mesabi Range and shipping it down the Great Lakes to the steel mills in America's industrial heartland. The house at 2105 East Superior had been erected in the 1890s and was once the home of Marcus Lafayette Fay, a native-born Canadian who discovered the Minorca and Chisholm mines on the Mesabi Range and a political figure who served one term as mayor of Virginia during its iron-mining heyday shortly after the turn of the century.

One of the biggest changes Olsen has seen in her nearly 20 years in the hearing aid business has been the revolution in technology brought about primarily by America's move into space. In earlier years the hearing impaired were forced to wear cumbersome battery packs on their legs and a microphone strapped to their chest. But the development of light-weight batteries for America's Mercury and Apollo space programs led to applications in many other fields, including audiology. Today a hearing aid wearer can be accommodated with a unit that fits in the ear or ear canal and carries battery, microphone, and amplifier in a

This beautiful old Victorian house, at 2105 East Superior Street in Duluth, is the home of the Arrowhead Hearing Aid Center.

———

package that weighs a few ounces. And the current electronics revolution is leading to the development of sophisticated amplification and testing equipment that was unheard-of when Louise Olsen started Arrowhead Hearing Aid Center in 1964.

———

The original beauty of the firm's home is evident in this door and transom of leaded and stained glass.

MARINE IRON AND SHIP BUILDING COMPANY

In the late 1970s Duluthians grew accustomed to seeing the U.S. Coast Guard cutter *Sundew* plying the harbor and the nearby waters of Lake Superior. What many younger Duluthians didn't know, however, was that the *Sundew* and 20 other similar cutters were built during World War II in the Marine Iron and Ship Building yards at 11th Avenue West and Railroad Street.

steamer *Richard Reiss*, altered the steamer *Montauk*, and built the tender *Maple*.

It was the Japanese attack on Pearl Harbor that propelled Marine Iron into its period of greatest activity. In the four years that the war raged overseas, Marine Iron built 21 Coast Guard cutters, three net tenders, and six tankers. The yards were a beehive of activity, with crews working around the clock. In 1943 Marine Iron was capable of launching cutters seven weeks after the keel was laid; in one three-month period the *Hornbeam, Redbud, Sassafras, Spar,* and *Sedge* steamed out of the yards bound for duty. *Hornbeam* and *Spar* would both make news in the postwar years, the *Spar* by circumnavigating North America in 1957 and the *Hornbeam* by being the first

industrial plumbing firm, had subcontracted the piping work for ships built at Marine Iron during the war. In 1960 Meierhoff sold Marine Iron's dry docks and tugs to Fraser Shipyards in nearby Superior, Wisconsin, and another firm, Cutler-Magner, took over the Marine Iron shipyard site at 11th Avenue West.

Meierhoff purchased the Marshall-Wells Building on Lake Avenue South in the 1960s and moved the offices of Marine Iron to the renamed Meierhoff Building. Since that time the corporation, Marine Iron, pri-

---

The Marine Iron shipyard participated in the accelerated activity that visited the port's shipbuilding industry during World War I.

The yards themselves dated to 1880, when Napoleon Grignon started a ship-repair business at the foot of Buchanan Street and Lake Avenue. Napoleon's nephew, Peter Grignon, took over the business in 1905, by which time the yards were primarily repairing boats—like the passenger steamer *America*, which entered local lore when she foundered off Isle Royale in 1928. The company participated in the prosperity that visited the port's shipbuilding industry during World War I, repairing lake vessels in its yards and making artillery shells under government contract.

Like most of the other shipyards in the harbor, Marine Iron watched business decline after the Armistice was signed in 1918. But with the only floating dry dock at the Head of the Lakes, Marine Iron retained enough business to help it weather the Depression in the between-war years. The firm, which employed close to 100 men throughout the period, constructed derricks for the U.S. government, overhauled the

rescue vessel to reach the stricken *Andrea Doria* in 1956.

Defense contracts again dried up after the war, and Marine Iron was reduced to building farm wagons. The firm was purchased by a group of 10 Duluthians, including Marvin Meierhoff. Meierhoff's Modern Constructors, a Duluth-based

marily employs boilermakers to do boiler repair and steel fabricating.

In 1943 Marine Iron was a beehive of activity brought on by World War II. The firm built Coast Guard cutters, some of which are still plying the waters of Lake Superior today.

MAIN HURDMAN

When A.O. Grover opened a one-man accounting office in Duluth's First Federal Savings Building in 1917, America was just being introduced to the rigors of World War I, and federal income tax was only four years old. Today the successor to the Grover firm is the Duluth office of Main Hurdman, an international accounting firm with 80 offices in the United States and full-service coverage in 70 countries. The Duluth office's newest partner-in-charge is Jack A. Sellwood.

The Grover firm did business in the First Federal Savings Building for 57 years, 40 of them on the same floor, recalled recently retired partner-in-charge Earl J. Lockhart. For the first five years A.O. Grover ran the office by himself. In 1922 Grover's son Irving graduated from law school in St. Paul and joined his father in the Duluth practice. The two partners didn't even have a secretary, and it was two years before a third person joined Grover and Grover. Virgil J. Pedrizetti, a native of Piedmont, Italy, came on board in 1924. By 1930 he was a partner in the firm of Grover, Pedrizetti and Co.

At about the same time, two young Duluth accountants named Lawrence Graving and Karl Honigman were studying for the CPA examination. In 1933, at the height of the Depression, the two men passed the test and received their certificates. The following year they opened the firm of Graving and Honigman, sealing the deal with a handshake.

At the Grover and Pedrizetti firm, World War II was a time of change and upheaval. Ray Grover, another of A.O. Grover's sons,

---

Jack A. Sellwood, Duluth office partner-in-charge.

A.O. Grover, founding partner of the Duluth office of Main Hurdman.

---

joined the firm as an employee in 1936. Founder A.O. Grover died in 1941, and his son Irving left the partnership the next year to take an executive position with Northern Drug Company. The firm changed its name to V.J. Pedrizetti and Co., and many of the employees were called to serve their country during the war.

The postwar period brought a return of the Grover name to the partnership. Ray Grover rejoined the firm in 1946. Three years later Duluth native Earl J. Lockhart returned to the Twin Ports from Minneapolis and joined the firm. In 1952 Grover and Lockhart were named partners.

The Graving and Honigman firm merged with Pedrizetti, Grover and Lockhart in 1966, and three years later the Duluth firm merged with Main Lafrentz. Pedrizetti, Graving, and Honigman all retired within three years of the Main Lafrentz merger, and the remaining partners moved the company's offices to the seventh floor of the Missabe Building two blocks away.

Today the organization is the Duluth office of Main Hurdman, a major national accounting firm created by merger in 1979. But the Duluth office is the direct descendant of that one-man operation founded by A.O. Grover during World War I.

M&K STORES

When Norwegian immigrant Sievert Morterud opened a retail clothing store at 21st Avenue West and Superior Street in 1884, Duluth was on the threshold of becoming the major iron ore shipping port in the United States. That same year the rich iron ore of Minnesota's Vermilion and Mesabi iron ranges would be hauled down to the docks of West End for transport down the Great Lakes.

The neighborhood where Sievert Morterud located his clothing store in 1884—and where M&K Stores is located today, less than a city block from the original location—became the major industrial area of the Twin Ports. Besides the docks, there were manufacturing plants, mills, and shipyards, and several generations of immigrant workmen and their families bought their clothes at M&K.

Sievert Morterud's youngest brother, Peter, followed his sibling to Duluth from the family farm in Wisconsin and joined him in the business. In 1908 the Norwegian brothers were joined by Matt Koneczny, a Polish immigrant to Duluth. The store name was changed to Morterud & Koneczny, and the business located a block down the street at 20th Avenue West and Superior. Just before World War I, Nelson Knitting Mills constructed a brick building on the original site at 21st Avenue West, and Morterud & Koneczny moved back as the mill's prime tenant. It wasn't until 1946 that M&K moved again, this time to 2016 West Superior.

Matt Koneczny bought out the Morterud's, and he and his son Ed ran M&K until Matt's death in the early 1950s. Ed Koneczny bought the store from his father's estate, selling out in 1966 to Sid Adelson. Born and raised in the east end of Duluth, Adelson's family was involved in the grocery business in the Twin Ports and northeastern Minnesota for many years. An employee of Fashion Wagon for 21 years, Adelson had worked with most of the major textile and apparel mills when he purchased M&K, at which time a change was begun from a conservative workingman's store, to an updated operation and one of northern Minnesota's leading fashion apparel houses. In 1972 the new owner bought the former JCPenney store at 2010 West Superior Street as the new quarters of M&K. A line of ladies' apparel was added, and M&K began an expansion program that saw stores opened in Virginia, Hibbing, Cloquet, and nearby Superior, Wisconsin.

The original M&K store, located in the heart of what remains a vibrant retail shopping district on West Superior Street, still caters to the grandsons and granddaughters of the Polish, Italian, Finnish, Yugoslav, and Scandinavian immigrants who built Duluth's industrial might. And the original store—the shop Sievert Morterud first opened almost 100 years ago—has been recreated into an innovative 1890s Duluth street scene at Depot Square, in the Lake Superior Museum of Transportation downtown.

———

M&K's original store was located at 2101 West Superior Street, less than a city block from where M&K Stores stands today.

COMO OIL COMPANY

World War II was just over when Brainerd native Myles Hall returned to Duluth, where he had started his business career in the late 1930s after graduating from college. In January 1946 Hall, who had spent the war years as a special agent for the FBI in Minnesota and on the West Coast, joined Duluth businessmen Clifford Donaghy and Oscar Mathisen in buying Western Fuel Company.

Western Fuel had been owned out of Minneapolis, and the venture was small, with three gas stations, two tank trucks, and a handful of heating-oil customers. The new owners renamed it Como Oil Company, a name that had no real significance but one that manager Hall felt would be easy for customers to remember and for him to market. Hall set up Como's offices in a little two-story converted gas station at 5 West Commerce Street.

By 1948 the fledgling Como Oil was selling about two million gallons of petroleum products a year, equally split between motor gasoline and heating fuel. But pent-up demand from all the veterans returning to civilian life and supply problems caused petroleum shortages in many parts of the country that year. Independent distributors were hit particularly hard, and in 1949 Como signed on with Phillips Petroleum, a partnership that has continued for 34 years.

Como had merged with Mitchell Oil and Fuel Company by 1957, with Hall as president and John Mitchell as vice-president. From new offices at 416 East Superior (in the first two-story building in Duluth) the firm operated 35 filling stations, five bulk plants, 23 fuel oil trucks, and a propane storage plant near Nopeming. Seven years later Como bought and refurbished an old facility at 749 East Superior. With a tile and glass facade, the structure contained Como's offices and a two-bay service station.

The '60s and '70s saw further expansion of Como's business and reputation. Hall

Como's original location, at 5 West Commerce Street.

———

served as the youngest president of the Northwest Petroleum Association before going on to serve a term as president of the National Oil Jobbers Association in 1963-1964. Como, as a distributor of propane gas from Duluth to the Canadian border, built propane storage plants in Two Harbors and Grand Marais.

The Arab oil embargo and other petroleum supply disruptions of the '70s pointed Como Oil on the road to diversification. As the decade of the '80s dawned, the firm still had its long-established service station, propane, and fuel-oil business. But Como had added a new bulk lubricating-oil business, a restaurant, and a major rent-a-car franchise for the Duluth area while continuing its role as petroleum products distributor for northeastern Minnesota and northwestern Wisconsin.

WEBC RADIO

Duluthians were accustomed to receiving more than their share of network radio news in the late 1920s. WEBC, the NBC affiliate in the Twin Ports, offered listeners both the network's Red and Blue services—primarily because President Calvin Coolidge spent much of his summers at the Cedar Island Lodge on the Brule River just outside neighboring Superior, Wisconsin. For the Republican National Convention in 1928, in fact, WEBC offered to set up remote broadcasting facilities in case "Silent Cal" decided to address the delegates.

By 1928 WEBC was four years old and broadcasting on 1,000 watts across the northland. Started by U.S. Navy veteran Walter C. Bridges (hence the W, B, and C of the call letters) at his home in Superior in 1924, the fledgling station moved across the St. Louis River to offices in Duluth's Spalding Hotel in 1928. Along the way, the station had been incorporated as Head of the Lakes Broadcasting, with the Duluth *News Tribune*, Morgan Murphy's *Superior Evening Telegram*, and the Weyerhaeuser family of St. Paul as partial partners in the venture.

Through the Great Depression WEBC essentially had the Duluth radio market all to itself. By 1938 the station's offices sported four separate studios and broadcasts from both the NBC and CBS radio networks. The station's Arrowhead network blanketed Duluth and surrounding counties in Minnesota and Wisconsin, and early in 1941 the Federal Communications Commission increased the station's transmission capacity to 5,000 watts, both day and night. Announcers such as James Payton, Jack Delahunt, and Hale Byers had devoted listeners from Cloquet up across the Mesabi Iron Range to the North Shore.

WEBC became involved with the race to bring television to the Twin Ports after World War II. The radio station changed its frequency to 560 kilocycles (from 1,320 kilocycles, where it had been for decades) in 1955, and three years later the station was sold to a West Virginia radio station owner, the first of a series of ownership changes WEBC was to undergo in the next two decades. WMT-AM Television of Cedar Rapids, Iowa, bought the station in 1960, only to sell it to Red Owl Stores in 1965. Red Owl was purchased by Gamble-Skogmo in 1968, but the grocery chain was required to divest its broadcast properties, selling WEBC and several other Upper Midwest Stations to the Park Broadcasting Company of Ithaca, New York. Because of FCC rules limiting the number of stations a company can own at one time, Park sold WEBC to Midwest Radio, Inc., of Fargo, North Dakota, in 1976.

As the decade of the 1980s gets under way, WEBC remains a fixture on the AM radio dial, the oldest, continuous broadcast outlet in the Twin Ports.

————

A WEBC disc jockey broadcasts over the oldest, continuous broadcast outlet in the Twin Ports, circa 1965.

LAKE HAVEN MANOR

What is today one of the larger nursing homes in the Twin Ports started as a favor for a vacationing Duluth family. One summer day in 1949, Ted and Wilhelmina Hargest and her mother, Emma Gardner, were asked to care for the elderly grandmother of neighbors while the family took a short vacation. The trio took the elderly woman into their home on Park Point, and within several weeks had accepted two more elderly guests.

Then-administrator Wilhelmina Hargest remembers that by the end of that first summer, the patient load at the Hargest home at 2833 Lake Avenue South had become so great that the Hargests and her mother were forced to move into the house next door. And that was for fewer than a dozen patients.

Three years later the Hargests located new, expanded quarters for their Lake Haven nursing home. In 1952 they moved into the second floor of the Weber Hospital building at 56th Avenue West. The Hargests estimated that they could care for 56 patients in the new facilities. Before 1953 was over they had reached that patient capacity and were negotiating for more room. In 1956 they took over the first floor at the clinic, and Lake Haven Manor was

able to increase its capacity to care for 82 residents. At this busy time, the home's present administrator, A.J. Newby, joined the staff and was a guiding hand through the growing pains of expansion.

The growth of the home and the staff continued during the two decades that Lake Haven Manor was located in the Weber Hospital property. But by the early 1970s the Hargests were committed to once again expanding the home. They looked at several sites around the city—including on the top of the hill overlooking the central business district—but eventually decided on a loca-

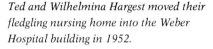

Ted and Wilhelmina Hargest moved their fledgling nursing home into the Weber Hospital building in 1952.

tion at 7700 Grand Avenue overlooking the beautiful St. Louis River. Construction took place throughout 1972, and in September of that year the staff and residents moved into the new quarters. The spacious brick and glass facility contains room for 132 residents, two large lobbies, three dining rooms, and a number of activity areas.

It is now a decade since Lake Haven Manor moved into its new quarters and 33 years since its start in a private home on Park Point. Barbara Hargest Korpela, the assistant administrator of the home, is the third generation of the family to be involved in Lake Haven Manor. The 132 residents—the oldest is 106—are cared for by a staff of 120. A great part of Lake Haven Manor's success in long-term care is due to its loyal, dedicated staff who sincerely care for the residents' welfare and happiness. The annual payroll exceeds one million dollars, and the home spends more than $800,000 a year just for food and other purchases. Lake Haven is at full capacity with a waiting list, and the home is investigating further expansion for the years ahead.

Today Lake Haven Manor is located in a spacious brick and glass facility at 7700 Grand Avenue.

ST. LUKE'S HOSPITAL

A century ago, the typhus bacillus was the most feared disease in America. Caused by tainted water supplies, typhoid fever periodically ravaged American communities such as Duluth. It wasn't until nearly the turn of the century that construction of modern plants to supply cities' water needs substantially lessened the danger of typhoid epidemics.

It was following one such typhoid outbreak in 1880-1881 that the Reverend Charles A. Cummings, the rector of St. Paul's Episcopal Church in Duluth, convinced the church trustees to back a subscription drive to buy an abandoned blacksmith shop at the corner of Third Avenue East and Superior Street. In November 1881 Cummings' efforts resulted in the opening of St. Luke's, the first hospital in Duluth.

The 12-bed hospital quickly outgrew its facilities and moved up the hill in 1884 to more spacious quarters at Second Avenue East and Fourth Street. The new 38-bed facility was to be in service until the turn of the century. During those early years, the doctors and staff continued to battle the typhoid menace; in the first seven years of St. Luke's existence, close to 40 percent of the hospital deaths were due to typhus, and the fact that the hospital was drawing its water supply from a contaminated source was a powerful spur to relocating St. Luke's to its present site (at Ninth Avenue East and

Many residents of Duluth remember St. Luke's Hospital's old west building (left), erected in 1902, and the center building, constructed in 1923. That same year another facility was completed on the upper side of the block, a nurses' dormitory that is still used as a residence and classrooms for the St. Luke's School of Nursing.

First Street) in 1900.

The opening of the new four-story hospital in 1902 more than doubled St. Luke's patient capacity to 95 beds. A second wing was added in 1926, and St. Luke's was expanded once again in 1950. In the late 1960s the hospital board authorized the replacement of the original 1902 structure with a new wing, and the hospital building program was completed for the time being with construction of a medical office complex catercorner to the main hospital facility in 1978.

A hospital is more than bricks and mortar. For more than 90 years St. Luke's has been educating nurses and, in conjunction with the University of Minnesota-Duluth and other area hospitals, it is now involved in educating doctors for northeastern Minnesota. Although the hospital retains the name given it by the trustees of St. Paul's Episcopal Church a century ago, St. Luke's has been governed by a nonsectarian board of directors since 1921.

Duluth has become the medical center for the people living in northeastern Minnesota and northwestern Wisconsin. With its Regional Trauma Center, full surgery facilities, and staff of more than 1,400 people, St. Luke's is positioned to carry on its tradition of meeting the health needs of the area.

St. Luke's Hospital of Duluth entered its second century of service to the community and region in 1982. It is a 400-bed general acute-care and teaching hospital that became the federally designated Regional Trauma Center in 1981. The east wing, added in the 1950s, is at right, and the west wing, completed in 1969, appears at left.

A. KEMP FISHERIES, INC.

It's a long way from Duluth, Minnesota, to Bethel, Alaska, but that's how far Louis Kemp went to expand the operations of A. Kemp Fisheries, Inc. But Kemp, the third generation of his family to head the firm, has retained its headquarters and some of its fish-processing operations in a local compound at 4832 West Superior Street.

Kemp's father and grandfather, Abe and Aaron Kemp, started the business in 1930. At that time, Duluth was a major fish-processing center on Lake Superior with some two dozen companies calling the Twin Ports home. The elder Kemps, post-World War I immigrants from Poland, bought fish from the commercial fishermen along Minnesota's North Shore, loaded the catch into a battered pick-up truck, and drove Lake Superior's bounty to the fresh-fish market in Chicago.

The Kemps branched out in the early 1940s, opening a processing plant on Garfield Avenue. In 1942 the company started processing imported dried cod for lutefish, a holiday staple for generations of the area's Scandinavian population. Changing economics, the increasing industrial pollution of Lake Superior, and the invasion of the Great Lakes by the sea lamprey—which was an unwanted visitor to fresh water during construction of the St. Lawrence Seaway—all contributed to a decline of the fisheries industry in Duluth during the 1950s. By that time Aaron Kemp had died, but Abe expanded the business to what was then Port Arthur, Ontario (now Thunder Bay), in the search for a new source of supply. Abe Kemp died in 1967 and left the business to son Louis.

Louis Kemp expanded into processing Lake Superior smelt when he purchased a plant at 59th Avenue West and the waterfront. That venture was cut short by a fire in February 1975. But in the meantime, Louis had taken the firm north and west, forming Kemp-Paulucci Seafoods to operate a fishing and processing barge out of the native settlement of Bethel. The other half of the partnership is the Paulucci family of Duluth, famous for starting Chun-King foods and Jeno's Pizza. In 1979 the firm bought an oil tanker and began converting it into a floating processor.

Like A. Kemp Fisheries, Inc., the newly rechristened *Bering Trader* got its start on the Great Lakes in the 1930s. The 290-foot *Traverse City Socony* began hauling fuel for Mobil Oil Corporation during the 1938 season on the Great Lakes. In 1962 she was rechristened the *Raymond J. Bushey* and hauled fuel around the Caribbean for 17 years. Since her purchase by Kemp, she has been completely remodeled into a floating processing factory, capable of producing more than 300,000 pounds of frozen Alaska salmon and herring per day. It is the largest American frozen floating processor.

It is, says Louis Kemp, the mothership concept introduced to Alaska waters. In 1982 the firm established its third operation in Alaska. This took over a freezer plant in Dillingham, Alaska, which processes herring and salmon. In 10 years' time Alaskan operations have grown to where A. Kemp Fisheries, Inc., now processes over 20 million pounds of fish from Alaska and is still growing. It is also an example of the new directions being taken by Duluth's A. Kemp Fisheries, Inc.

Like A. Kemp Fisheries, Inc., the rechristened Bering Trader *got its start on the Great Lakes in the 1930s.*

DIAMOND TOOL AND HORSESHOE CO.

When Swedish immigrants Otto Swanstrom, Frank Swanstrom, Ernest Peterson, Leonard Peterson, and A.R. Devohn opened a small manufacturing facility at 401 Lake Avenue South in 1908, motive power in the United States was provided by horses. So it was logical that the Diamond Calk should have a bright future. In those early days, Diamond made calks for horseshoes, removable cleats that helped horses gain traction in icy weather. In 1912 Swanstrom moved the business to 4632 Grand Avenue and began producing horseshoes as well as calks.

Diamond was forced to diversify its product line early on. Henry Ford's assembly line in Detroit seemed to spell the end of the horse-and-buggy era in America—and began to dry up the market for calked horseshoes. The firm started making railroad picks, entrenching tools, and wire cutters during World War I. Diamond introduced a line of adjustable wrenches for Henry Ford's still-newfangled automobile market in 1920. The company employed 145 men at its Grand Avenue plant and a staff of six salesmen handled marketing duties. In 1929 Diamond completed a 22,000-square-foot addition to the Grand Avenue factory.

Otto Swanstrom and his brother Frank never really abandoned their original product line. The company bought the Minnesota Horseshoe Calk Company in 1922. Diamond also began the manufacture of pitching horseshoes, a line that is still pro-

duced today. In 1926 a horseshoe and calk business in Toronto, Canada, was purchased.

Throughout the 1930s Diamond continued to diversify its product line, and when the United States was plunged into World War II, the firm geared up to manufacture a variety of special tools. It produced tank-track adjustors, automotive wrenches, and forgings for other manufacturers. Diamond's work force jumped to 500, and each month the company consumed 500 tons of steel made at the nearby Morgan Park mill of U.S. Steel. Before the

Shown here is Diamond's oldest known advertisement with Otto Swanstrom, at left, and Frank Swanstrom, at right.

war was over, Diamond was awarded two of the prestigious Army/Navy "E" Awards.

Otto Swanstrom died in 1945; his brother Frank succeeded him as president until his death in 1952. The manufacture of hand tools for the industrial, automotive, and home repair markets became far more important in the postwar years. So, under the leadership of John Swanstrom in 1958, the firm changed its name to Diamond Tool and Horseshoe Co. to reflect the predominance of tools to the industry. A major resurgence of the horseshoe business began for Diamond in 1965 as other major producers gave up this field and Diamond expanded its line and capacity.

In 1982 the firm—which by then

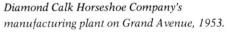

Diamond Calk Horseshoe Company's manufacturing plant on Grand Avenue, 1953.

employed 660 workers—was purchased by the Triangle Corporation of Stamford, Connecticut. Triangle announced its intention to purchase new equipment to further modernize and expand Diamond's Duluth manufacturing facility. This marriage brought about a close alliance with Triangle's other subsidiaries, Utica Tool Company, Inc., Triangle International, Inc., and Miller Special Tools, and added great strength to all in what had become a most competitive world market.

The company's senior Duluth management staff: (front row, left to right) George Clarke, R. William Metzger, Jim Davis, Shirley Kaczmark, Vic Tapper, and Rod Hietala; (back row, left to right) Len Bubacz, Harry Gee, Don Gates, Ben Porschet, and Pat Russell. Not shown is Tony Tokarczyk.

JOHNSON MORTUARY

World War I was in its waning days in May 1918 and Duluth was enjoying the prosperity of the wartime economy when Frank A. Johnson and his son established a mortuary business at 319 East Superior Street.

A native of Sweden, Frank Johnson had come to the United States in the early 1880s at the age of 19 and traveled to Minneapolis where he joined a brother who had emigrated to Minnesota several years before. The two brothers had worked in the then-booming white pine lumber business in the Twin Cities for three years when Frank Johnson started a retail lumber business in the small town of Evansville, Minnesota.

Johnson's oldest son, Edwin, was born in Evansville in 1888. In 1896 the family moved to Elbow Lake, Minnesota, where Frank Johnson was a hardware merchant and lumberman for two decades. Edwin graduated from high school in Elbow Lake and went off to the Twin Cities for college, attending Minnesota College in Minneapolis

for two years and then enrolling in the 1908 embalming course at the University of Minnesota. After successfully completing the course, Edwin Johnson worked for funeral homes in Duluth and then sold equipment for a Minneapolis mortuary supply firm. A decade after graduating from college, Edwin Johnson went into partnership with his father in the business of F.A. Johnson & Son, Funeral Directors.

Duluth was a growing industrial city with room for entrepreneurs providing needed services. Tragically, the service provided by F.A. Johnson & Son would come into great demand before the year was out. Duluth was hit hard by the influenza epidemic that swept the nation that year, and in October the area was devastated by forest fires with a resulting loss of life estimated at close to 1,000 persons.

The father-son partnership purchased the Victorian home of lumber baron Francis Tims at 514 East Third Street in 1921. Located in the posh Ashtabula Heights neighborhood of Duluth, the new home of F.A. Johnson & Son has served as the company's headquarters for more than 60 years. The early 1920s were a time of growth for

the new business as Edwin's brothers Franklin, Carroll, and Maynard joined the partnership. Edwin's son, Warren, joined the firm in 1936.

The company remained in the Johnson family until 1978, when it was purchased by Bernard Kalkbrenner. A native Duluthian, Kalkbrenner graduated from a local high school and in 1965 received an associate of arts degree in mortuary science from the University of Minnesota. He worked in St. Paul for 13 years before returning to Duluth to purchase Johnson Mortuary.

Since that time, Kalkbrenner has sold shares in the business to employees Arlo Danielson, Paul Bergquist, and Dennis Anderson. Although the founding family is no longer associated with the day-to-day operation of the business, Johnson Mortuary perpetuates their name in the Duluth business community.

————

F.A. Johnson & Son, Funeral Directors, purchased the Victorian home of lumber baron Francis Tims at 514 East Third Street in 1921. The firm is still located there today.

CRAWFORD FUNERAL SERVICE

When James L. Crawford arrived in the St. Louis River town of Cloquet, Minnesota, in 1881, he was one of millions of his fellow countrymen who had left their native Ireland to seek opportunity in America. Born in Omagh near Belfast in 1863, Crawford established himself in the general merchandise business in the lumber mill town of Cloquet. Six years later he moved to Minneapolis where he learned the undertaking business with N.F. Warner & Company. Crawford later relocated to the booming port city of Duluth in 1889, just three years before the Merritt family started shipping the rich, red iron ore of the Mesabi Range through the Twin Ports. He opened the first drugstore in West Duluth.

Later that year Crawford went into business with M.J. Durkan, a St. Paul mortician he had met in the Twin Cities. The two men bought out the Duluth firm of Donnelly & Sons, Undertakers, on Second Avenue West and opened M.J. Durkan & Company. At the turn of the century the firm changed its name to Durkan & Crawford, and in 1910 James Crawford bought out his partner. Crawford moved the mortuary from Second Avenue West, its location for almost a quarter-century, to a new site at 202 West Second Street in 1912. The second generation of the family, James' son, William Ward Crawford, entered the business two years later after attending the Wharton School of Finance at the University of

Pennsylvania. The firm changed its name to J.L. Crawford & Son at that time.

The next major change came in 1922, when J.L. Crawford & Son purchased a site at Second Avenue East and Second Street and commenced construction on one of the most modern mortuary facilities in the Upper Midwest. Duluth architect Carl E. Nystrom drew the plans for the two-story Georgian-style building and George H. Lounsberry was awarded the general construction contract.

Building costs totaled $100,000, including the then-considerable sum of $11,000 just for excavation. The structure was roofed in Spanish tile, had an electric elevator in the rear, and contained a funeral chapel with seating capacity of 300. J.L. Crawford & Son completed the expansion program with the purchase of an entire fleet of Cadillac motor cars, including two hearses, a casket car, and a touring car for

This horse-drawn funeral procession was photographed on Mesaba Avenue, Duluth, early in this century.

———

pallbearers. Dr. Noble Elderkin, pastor of the Pilgrim Congregational Church, gave the dedication address for the new mortuary at ceremonies held under the auspices of the Duluth Ministerial Association on October 6, 1923.

James L. Crawford was active in the firm until his death in 1941. By that time, a third generation of Crawfords had entered the family business. James P. Crawford, William's son, graduated from the Mortuary Science School at the University of Minnesota in 1941. He then returned to Duluth, but joined the U.S. Army and served in the Quartermaster Corps in the European Theater of Operations until 1946. He joined his father in the company that year, a partnership that remained until William Crawford's death in 1979 at the age of 89.

By the early 1980s a fourth generation of Crawfords had joined the enterprise. Joan Crawford Young's participation in Crawford Funeral Service extends her family's involvement in the Duluth funeral business almost to the century mark.

———

J.L. Crawford & Son commenced construction on one of the most modern mortuary facilities in the Upper Midwest in 1922. The two-story Georgian-style building was roofed in Spanish tile, had an electric elevator in the rear, and contained a funeral chapel with a seating capacity of 300.

MILLER-DWAN MEDICAL CENTER

Andreas M. Miller might well have been amazed by the trials that attended the birth of the hospital that bears his name. Miller, a wealthy financier and mayor of Duluth in 1877, left the city $600,000 when he died in 1917. The money was to be used for the construction of a hospital for the needy sick and the helpless poor of the Twin Ports, a fitting memorial for the Duluth businessman. From the start, however, there were questions of whether or not the proposed Miller hospital could accept paying patients. In addition, the city council wrestled with the question of tapping the trust fund for operation of the proposed hospital once it was built.

In 1930 hospital consultant Dr. William Walsh reported to the council that there was a 200-bed shortage in Duluth. A district court ruled that the hospital could accept patients for pay, and a board of trustees was appointed the next year. In 1932, 15 years after Miller's death, construction finally began on a site located at Fifth Avenue East and Second Street. By the time the new five-story Miller Memorial Hospital opened its doors during National Hospital Week in May 1934, the cost of the land, building, and furnishings totaled $266,000. But in the intervening years, the money left in trust by Miller had been drawing interest and dividends so that the original $600,000 had grown to just over one million dollars. After all the construction bills were deducted, the new Miller Memorial Hospital had $745,000 in its trust fund.

By August of that first year of operation there were 84 physicians on the staff and 189 new patients had been admitted. Within five years Miller Memorial was admitting over 800 new patients annually.

Miller Memorial completed its first quarter-century in operation in 1959, and the board of trustees began to lay the groundwork for expansion of the facilities. The first 25 years saw the hospital staff treat some 25,000 patients and perform 10,000 operations. During the first year of the second quarter-century, a district court ruled that the hospital could utilize the trust funds to enlarge its facilities.

The 1960s were exciting years at Miller Memorial. A land purchase and exchange between the Duluth Rehabilitation Center and the hospital paved the way for the establishment of the Polinsky Rehabilitation Center, adjacent to the hospital. In October 1968 ground was broken for a $7.4-million, eight-story addition. The hospital was able to draw upon private gifts for more than half that amount, $1.6 million from the Miller Trust, and $2.4 million from Mrs. Mary Dwan, a former board member. In appreciation and recognition of the generous support of Mrs. Dwan, the name Miller-Dwan was adopted in 1971.

Since that time, Miller-Dwan Medical Center has concentrated on expanding its role as a speciality medical center. Speciality services include a kidney dialysis unit, burn center, radiation therapy center, arthritis treatment center, mental health services, general surgical services, and an alcohol and chemical dependency treatment facility—Miller-Dwan West.

Begun in 1934 from money left to the city by Andreas M. Miller, a former mayor of Duluth, the hospital was renamed Miller-Dwan Medical Center in appreciation of the generous support of former board member Mrs. Mary Dwan.

PIONEER NATIONAL BANK OF DULUTH

The history of Pioneer National Bank is more than a story of bricks and mortar, debits and credits, checking accounts and savings deposits. It is also the story of a Duluth family that has been active in Twin Ports banking circles for four generations spanning the past century and a quarter.

Brothers Hamilton H. Peyton and John N. Peyton started the Citizens State Bank on Central Avenue, West Duluth, in 1912. The western portion of the Zenith City was a bastion of industrial might in that era, populated by factories, docks, and mills. Community leaders lived with the expectation that the U.S. Steel mill in the nearby western suburb of Morgan Park would soon begin casting ingots. The two Peyton brothers borrowed money from their father to start their bank and take advantage of the booming economic conditions.

By that time the elder Hamilton M. Peyton had been involved in Twin Ports banking and other business ventures for more than a half-century. A native of Geneva, New York, he had come to nearby Superior, Wisconsin, in 1857 and had established the first private bank at the Head of the Lakes. Peyton also was involved in the lumber, wholesale grocery, and shipping industries. In 1879 he reorganized the Duluth Savings Bank—the only area financial institution to survive the disastrous bank panic of 1873—as the American Exchange Bank. Later renamed the American Exchange National Bank, it was merged with First National Bank in 1929 to become the First and American National Bank.

Hamilton M. Peyton's sons proved to be successful bankers in their own right, securing a national bank charter for Citizens State in 1927 and renaming the firm Pioneer National Bank. In 1933—a time of trial and tribulation for the banking industry in Minnesota—John N. Peyton was appointed Minnesota Commissioner of Banks by Governor Floyd B. Olson and sold his share in Pioneer National to his brother. The new banking commissioner, a Republican, expressed reservations to the radical Farmer-Labor governor about accepting the appointment. "You worry about the banks, I'll worry about the politics," family tradition has Olson replying to the Duluth banker. John N. Peyton was later named chairman of the Federal Reserve Bank in Minneapolis.

The younger Hamilton H. Peyton died in 1957 and his son, Newton H. Peyton, assumed control of Pioneer National. That same year the bank, which had been in the same facility since the Citizens State years, purchased the Wheiland Hardware Building next door, moved in, and remodeled the quarters. The relocation effectively tripled the bank's space and allowed it to add one of the first drive-up windows in Duluth.

The great-grandson of Hamilton M. Peyton, John E. Peyton became the fourth generation of the family to head a Twin Ports bank when he was elected president of Pioneer National in 1973. In 1983 he continued to head the bank with deposits of over $13 million, a far cry from the $100,000 capital that the bank began with in 1912. Today the bank, located at 331 North Central Avenue, has a completely new exterior, employs 18 people, and is enjoying what its management considers excellent growth.

And the Peyton family of Duluth continues its 125-year association with banking at the Head of the Lakes.

———

Begun in 1912 as the Citizens State Bank and located on Central Avenue in West Duluth, the institution was renamed the Pioneer National Bank in 1927.

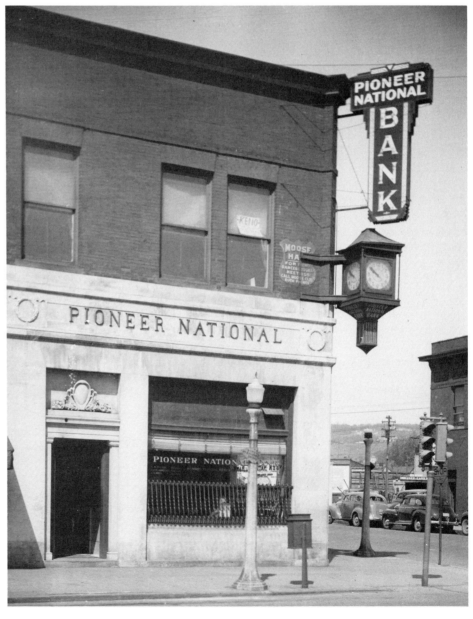

INDUSTRIAL WELDORS & MACHINISTS, INC.

Business conditions in the iron mining industry of northeastern Minnesota were not exactly booming in 1952, when James Arthur Abernethy founded Industrial Weldors & Machinists in a small shop at 350 South First Avenue East. The Korean War was stalemated, and the nation was locked in the grip of an industry-wide steel strike. Abernethy and partner E.V. Lindberg had correctly assessed the potential for welding, fabrication, and machine work needed by the then-emerging taconite industry on the nearby Mesabi Iron Range. Over the next three decades the Duluth firm did work for all of the Mesabi Range taconite producers, deriving as much as 70 percent of its sales from the industry.

Born on April 11, 1920, in Duluth, Minnesota, James Abernethy is the son of Thomas Wesley and Mary (Binane) Abernethy. His father, who was born in Toronto, Ontario, Canada, died in 1937. Mary Binane also was born in Duluth.

Abernethy attended Central High School in Duluth, working during the summers while he was a student. During September 1940 he became employed by the Zenith Dredge Company, working as foreman on the construction of the *Woodrush* and other U.S. Coast Guard cutters built in Duluth.

From 1943 to 1945 Abernethy served in the U.S. Navy in the South Pacific. A member of a Naval aircraft squadron, he was a crew member of Pacific Patrols. Following his military service he returned to Duluth, where he joined the Abernethy Iron Works. He worked as a machinist with that firm until 1952, when he founded Industrial Weldors & Machinists with his partner.

Faced with the need for expansion of its cramped facilities on South First Avenue East, in 1956 the firm purchased a new facility located on the bayfront at 1003 Minnesota Avenue, on Park Point. That same year Industrial Weldors & Machinists purchased the old Biwabik Mine Building near Biwabik from Pickands Mather & Company because major contracts with the taconite firms were handled more easily from a location on the iron range. As the taconite industry expanded in northeastern

James A. Abernethy—founder and chairman of Industrial Weldors & Machinists.

Minnesota after the mid-1950s, Industrial Weldors & Machinists secured contracts for ore car repair and assembly of huge mining trucks.

E.V. Lindberg sold his share in the business to Abernethy in 1964. Seven years later the firm further expanded on the iron range when it purchased the old Danube Mine location at Bovey from Pickands Mather & Company, where ore cars were rebuilt and fabrication carried on until a rail spur abandonment later in the decade forced Industrial Weldors to close the site.

By 1976 the Duluth fabrication and machining firm employed some 80 persons and serviced industrial clients throughout

the region. But disaster struck the following year. A major fire destroyed the company's Park Point headquarters. Fortunately, Industrial Weldors & Machinists had purchased the old Globe Iron Works site at 3902 Oneota Street from Abernethy's uncles a few years before for possible expansion, and it was able to move to the west end location and quickly resume business. After the fire the property was converted into a marina. Abernethy recalls that the firm's business with the local taconite companies wasn't seriously affected by the fire; the range was shut down for most of the last half of 1977 by a steelworkers' strike.

James Abernethy was married to Patricia Ann Glennie of Duluth, the daughter of Peter and Elizabeth Glennie, on May 15, 1942. Mr. and Mrs. Abernethy are the parents of four sons: Donald James, Charles Patrick (deceased), Ronald Bruce, and Scott Allan. They also have five grandchildren: Randall Scott, Dawn Patricia, Richard James, Robert Calvin, and Tara Lyn. James Abernethy has a cousin in West Germany by the name of Helmut Schmidt, who was chancellor of that country until late 1982.

James Abernethy turned the business over to his three sons, Don, Ron, and Scott in 1982, but remains active as its chairman of the board.

This scenic Park Point locale was the headquarters for Industrial Weldors & Machinists prior to a disastrous fire in 1977. Since that time the firm has been at 3902 Oneota Street. It currently maintains a marina at the former Park Point headquarters.

RADISSON HOTEL CORPORATION

When the Radisson Duluth Hotel opened its doors the last week of May 1970, it was the first new hotel built in the Twin Ports in 45 years. It was also the second hotel for the expansion-minded Radisson Hotel Corporation of Minneapolis, which saw the growing Duluth-Superior area as an important new market.

Duluth in 1970 was experiencing one of its periodic booms and the city needed a first-class hotel in the downtown area as a cornerstone to serve its tourism and convention economy. Just six years before, Minnesota voters had passed the "Taconite Amendment," and development of that strategic industry was forging ahead. In Duluth, the city had recently built a new arena-auditorium complex on the bayfront and other downtown developments were under study.

———

Joining here in 1975 at a historic five-year anniversary party for the Radisson Duluth Hotel were Curtis L. Carlson (right), board chairman of the Minneapolis-based Radisson Hotel Corporation, and Robert Prescott, prominent Duluth businessman and president of Greysolon Mall Corporation, which owns the hotel.

The 16-story Radisson Duluth Hotel features a striking circular tower, which became an immediate landmark in the Duluth skyline. Special amenities of the hotel include a glass-enclosed, revolving rooftop restaurant which offers diners a commanding view of downtown Duluth and the city's famous harbor. Meeting facilities, cocktail lounges, and a swimming pool are among the other attractions of the hotel.

Built at a cost of almost $4 million, the Radisson Duluth Hotel is located at the corner of Fifth Avenue West and Superior Street. It was the first all-electric hotel in the state of Minnesota and it was named after one of the earliest explorers in the Lake Superior area, French Canadian voyageur Pierre Esprit Radisson.

The hotel is managed by Radisson Hotel Corporation, one of the subsidiaries of Carlson Companies, Inc., of Minneapolis. The hotel and land upon which it is located are owned by Greysolon Mall Corporation, a consortium of Duluth businesses formed to finance the project.

This "marriage" of local hotel ownership with professional management has been cited as one of the key ingredients in the success of the Radisson Duluth Hotel through the years. Involving local business and civic leadership in the ownership of the hotel guarantees their vested interest in the success of the project.

In Duluth the Radisson Hotel proved so successful that it was expanded with a major addition in 1977. This project added 66 new guest rooms and suites, bringing the total number of rooms in the hotel to 268. The indoor swimming pool was renovated as a focal point of family recreational activity for visiting guests.

The location of the 268-room hotel is on a site steeped in Duluth Hotel tradition; just a block east on Superior Street was the site of the old Bay View Hotel, built in 1869. On the lower side of Superior Street at Fifth Avenue West—where the Duluth Public Library now stands—was the site of the Spalding Hotel, first built in 1889. In 1910 the 10-story, 150-room Holland Hotel was built in the same place as the Radisson. Meanwhile, the Radisson Hotel Corporation continued to expand to new locations around the United States and internationally. In 1982 this expansion reached across the Duluth harbor to Superior, Wisconsin, where a beautiful 115-room Radisson Inn opened on scenic Barker's Island. This resort-style property, with its 350-slip marina and numerous recreational facilities, provides an additional dimension of Radisson hospitality service to the Duluth-Superior area.

———

The striking circular tower of the Radisson Duluth Hotel offers guests a commanding view of the famous Lake Superior port. A revolving restaurant at the top of the hotel provides diners with a continuous changing view of the Duluth skyline and Lake Superior.

NOTES ON SOURCES

In compiling this brief history of the Zenith City of the Unsalted Seas, I have employed the archives and the periodic publications of: The St. Louis County Historical Society; The *Duluth News-Tribune* and the *Duluth Herald;* The Minnesota Historical Society; Northeast Minnesota Historical Center; St. Louis County Register of Deeds; The Duluth Public Library; The Douglas County (Wisconsin) Historical Museum; The Seaway Port Authority of Duluth.

I have also drawn upon the following books:

Davis, E.W. *Pioneering with Taconite.* St. Paul: Minnesota Historical Society, 1964.

DeKruif, Paul. *Seven Iron Men.* New York: Harcourt, Brace and Company, 1929.

Fedo, Michael W. *They Was Just Niggers.* Ontario, California: Brasch and Brasch Publishers, 1979.

Folwell, William Watts. *A History of Minnesota* (revised edition) St. Paul: Minnesota Historical Society, 1956.

Fritzen, John. *Historic Sites and Place Names of Minnesota's North Shore.* Duluth: St. Louis County Historical Society, 1974.

————. *History of North Shore Lumbering.* Duluth: St. Louis County Historical Society, 1968.

————. *The History of Fond du Lac and Jay Cooke Park.* Duluth: St. Louis County Historical Society, 1978.

Jackman, Sydney W., et al. (editors). *American Voyageur: The Journal of David Bates Douglass.* Marquette, Michigan: Northern Michigan University, 1969.

Kappler, Charles J. (editor). *Indian Affairs, Laws and Treaties,* vol. 2. Washington, D.C.: Government Printing Office, 1904.

Kimball, Gerald M. (editor and coordinator). *Duluth's Legacy: Volume 1, Architecture.* Duluth: City of Duluth, 1974.

King, Frank A. *The Missabe Road.* Duluth: Duluth, Missabe & Iron Range Railway, 1972.

Lydecker, Ryck. Pigboat: *The Story of the Whaleback.* Duluth: Sweetwater Press, 1973.

Lydecker, Ryck, and Sommer, Lawrence J. (editors). *Duluth: Sketches of the Past.* Duluth: American Revolution Bicentennial Commission, 1976.

MacDonald, Dora Mary. *This Is Duluth.* Duluth: Central High School Printing Department, 1950.

McKenney, Thomas L. *Sketches of a Tour to the Lakes* (facsimile reprint of 1827 edition). Minneapolis: Ross & Haines Incorporated, 1959.

Nute, Grace Lee. *Lake Superior.* Indianapolis and New York: Bobbs-Merrill Company, 1944.

Owen, David Dale. *Report of a Geological Survey of Wisconsin, Iowa and Minnesota.* Philadelphia: Congress of the United States, Lippincott, Grambo and Company, 1852.

Upham, Warren. *Minnesota Geographic Names* (reprint edition). St. Paul: Minnesota Historical Society, 1969.

Van Brunt, Walter. *Duluth and St. Louis County, Minnesota: Their Story and People,* vol. 1. Chicago and New York: The American Historical Society, 1921.

Warren, William W. *History of the Ojibway Nation* (reprint edition). Minneapolis: Ross & Haines Company, 1970.

Wolff, Julius F. Jr. *The Shipwrecks of Lake Superior.* Duluth: Lake Superior Marine Museum Association, 1979.

Woodbridge, Dwight E., and Pardee, John S. *History of Duluth and St. Louis County.* Chicago: C.F. Cooper & Company, 1910.

————. *For the Common Good: Finnish Immigrants and the Radical Response to Industrial America.* Wisconsin: Tyomies Society, Superior, 1977.

————. *The Minnesota Arrowhead Country* (compiled by the Writers' Program of the Work Projects Administration in Minnesota). Chicago: Albert Whitman and Company, 1941.

INDEX

A

A.M. Chisholm Museum 77
Aerial Lift Bridge *51*, 64, 74, 80, *81,*
87, 94, 95, 96
Agate Bay 21, 34
Air Defense Command, 515th 72
Aitkin, William A. 14
Alexander McDougall (steamer) 43
Alger, Horatio 75
Alger-Smith lumberyard 48, 60
Alletzhaeuser, Max 48
Allouez, Claude 15
Alworth, Marshall 60
American Board of Foreign Missions
14, 21
American Fur Company 13, 14, 21,
22, 49
American Legion 61
American Revolution 13
American Steel and Wire Company *59*
American Steel Barge Company 43, 44
Anchor Line 43
Anneke, Percy S. 84
Apostle Islands 17
Army Corps of Engineers 25, 31, 35,
51
Asp, Robert 79
Asseniboins Indians 10
Astor, John Jacob 13
Athletic Park 64

B

Babbitt (novel) 63
Banks and banking 72
Banning, Archibald T. 78
Banning, Margaret Culkin *78*
Bardon, James 24
Barnes-Duluth Shipbuilding Company
68
Barnes, Julius H. 60, 63, 69, 74
Barnes Riverside yard *69*
Barrett, R.H. 20, 23
Bartholdi, Frederic A. 47
Bartholdi, Raymond 47
Bates, David Douglass 14
Bayfield and St. Croix Railroad 39
Bayfield, Henry Woolsey 20
Beachey, Lincoln 64
Beaver *10*, 12
Beaver Bay 24
Beck, Isaac P. *29*
Belville 22
Berghult, C. Rudolph *67*
Bissell, Catherine 14, 21
Board of Trade 34
Boeing, Wilhelm 45
Boo, Ben 78
Booth and Sons, A. 49
Boulevard Drive 38, *52*
Boutwell, W.T. 15
Brandin, Betty (house of) *88*
Brandin, John (house of) *88*
Bray, W.T. 89
Brewery (Portland) 24

Bridgeman Russell Creamery 89
Brighton Beach *67*
Brown, Edwin 23
Brown, Zack 23
Brule, Etienne 10
Brule River 11
Bryan, William Jennings 52
Buchanan 20
Buchanan, James 20
Buffalo (Chief Ke-che-waish-ke) *17,*
45
Burnham, Daniel Hudson 6
Burnquist, J.A.A. 61

C

Cadotte, Charles *13*
Cadotte, Jean Baptiste 13
Camp Number One 27
Camp Thomas 50
Canadian Pacific Railroad 34
Canal Park Marine Museum 80, *87*
Carey, John R. 25, 26
Carlton, Reuben B. 15, 17, 22, 23, 25
Carnegie, Andrew 53
Cascade Park 36, *37, 86*
Cass, Lewis 14
Castle, Lewis G. 74
Cathedral of the Sacred Heart 44
Census 24, 35, 61, 77
Central Administration Building 86
Central High School 47, *49, 86*
Central Hockey Association 62
Champlain, Samuel de 10
Chaska (boat) 31, *32*
Chester Park 36, 37
Chicora (passenger ship) *21*
Chippewa Indians *9*, 10, 11, 12, 13, 14,
16, *17*, 18, *82, 83*
Christian Radich (sailboat) 76
Christiansen and Sons, H. 49
Christmas City of the North *80*
Christopher Columbus (whaleback) 43
Chun King Corporation 75
Churches 33, 49, 53, 57
"City Beautiful" movement 6
City Hall *6*, 63
City of Superior (steamboat) 22
Civic Center *6*, 63
Civil War 25
Clark House *30, 33*, 60
Clark House Creek *86*
Cloquet 66
Clure Public Marine Terminal 74
Clyde Iron Works 68
Cobb School 60
Coburn, R.G. 20
Colburn, Serenus 55
College of St. Scholastica 47, 55, 75
Congdon, Chester 60, 80
Connor's Point 22
Convent of the Sacred Heart 78
Cooke, Jay 21, 26, 27, 28, 30, 31, 32,
33, 34, 35, 57
Cooke's Bank 30

Coolerator 68
Copper mining 10, 15, 16, 23, 24, 25
Cowell's Addition to Duluth 20, 31
Cowell, William G. 20
Craggencroft Classical Institute 53
Craggencroft School 53
Crane, Richard Teller 82
Crooks, Ramsay 14
Culkin, William E. 63, 78
Culver, Joshua 23, 24, 26, 31
Cummings, J.A. 36

D

Dakota Indians *9*, 10, 21
Denfield, Robert E. 36, 47
Diescher, Samuel 46
Democratic-Farmer-Labor Party 75
Double Head Study-Indians (painting)
83
Drew, John 33
Duluth Aerial Ferry Bridge. *See* Aerial
Lift Bridge
Duluth Amphitheater 62
Duluth and Iron Range Railroad 24,
29, 34, 35, 63, 84, *85*
Duluth and Winnipeg Railroad 34
Duluth Arena-Auditorium 47, 75, 76,
90, 94
Duluth Bethel Society 33
Duluth Board of Education 49
Duluth Boat Club *62*, 74
Duluth Boat Clubhouse *64*
Duluth Boat Club rowers *63*
Duluth Brewing and Malting 61
Duluth Carriage Works
(advertisement) 38
Duluth Cathedral 36
Duluth Chamber of Commerce 67, 72,
74
Duluth City Council 33
Duluth Curling Club 47, *90*
Duluth Daily News (newspaper) 35,
36, 37, 40
Duluth Driving Park Association 47
Duluth Folk Festival 79, *90*
Duluth Herald (newspaper) 51, 55, 57,
61, 62, 64, 72
Duluth Herald and News-Tribune
building *87*
Duluth Hornets 62
Duluth Imperial Mill 42
Duluth Iron and Steel Company 33,
42, 55
Duluth, Mesabi & Northern Railroad
63
Duluth Minnesotian (newspaper) 28,
33
Duluth, Missabe & Iron Range
Railroad 39, 63, 70, *71, 84*
Duluth, Missabe & Northern Railway
48
Duluth Naval Reserve 72
Duluth News-Tribune (newspaper) 48,
54, 68, 74, 76, 79

Duluth Normal School 47, 53, 70
Duluth Playhouse 62, 77
Duluth Preservation Alliance 80
Duluth Public Library 75, 78
Duluth Public Library "Minnehaha"
window *82*
Duluth Ship Canal 32, 45
Duluth School Board 79
Duluth State Teachers College 70
Duluth Street Railway Company 35,
46
Duluth Summer Festival of the Arts *80*
Duluth-Superior Museum of
Transportation 77
Duluth-Superior Transit Company 65
Duluth Symphony Orchestra 63
Duluth Tribune (newspaper) 33, 46
Duluth Terminal Railway 40
Duluth Turnverein 48
Duluth Zoo 63

E

Eames, H.H. 25
Egan, James G. 30, 45
Eisenhower, Dwight D. 74
Elevator A 30, 31, 36
Elevator Q 34
Ellis, J.B. 23
Ely, Edmund Franklin 14, *21*, 22, 23,
24
Ely, Henry S. 31
Endion 22, 31
Enger, Bert J. 63, 65
Enger Memorial Tower *65*
Ericson, David 11, *85*
Erie Mining Company 72
Erikson, Leif 63
Euclid Hotel 55
E.W. Clark and Company 30

F

Famine of 1856 22
Farrell, James 66
Federal Building 6, 63
Federal Emergency Relief
Administration 64
Fero (tug) 32
Fighter Interceptor Squadron, 179th
72
Finnish American National Church 53
Fire Department 32, *33*
Firemen's Ball *33*
Fishing industry 14, *15*, 49, *50*, 75, 80,
91, 93
Fitger, August 84
Fitger Brewing 61, 84, *85*
Flaaten, Gustav *48*
Flaaten, Jens *48*
Fogg, Howard (watercolor) *84*
Fond du Lac Reservation *26*
Ford, Henry C. 23
Foster, Thomas Preston 27, 28, 33, 55,
79, 80
Franklin, Benjamin 13

Fremont 22, 32
French and Indian War 12
French River 16
French River mine 25
Fur trade 10, 12, 13, 14

G

Gateway Urban Renewal Project 75
Gaylord, Paul 42
George G. Hadley (ship) 43
Ginger (magazine) 84
Glensheen 80
Goldfine, Manley 76
Golrick, James 44
Goodhue, Bertram 88
Gott, Edwin 76
Grain trade 34, 61
Grand Army of the Republic 73;
    Joshua B. Culver Post 61
Grandma's Marathon 80
Grand Opera House 37, *38*
Grand Portage 12, 14, 17
Grassy Point 42
Great Depression 63, *64*, 65, 66, 67, 84
Great Northern Power Company 54
Greene Olsen Memorials, Inc. 92
Greysolon, Daniel, Sieur du Lhut 8, *9,*
    10, *11*, 12, 17, 73, 76
Griggs, Richard L. 66, 70

H

Hall, Lucien P. 49
Handy (schooner) 31, *32*
Hardy, Kate 53
Hardy School *53*
Heaney, Gerald W. 75
Hennepin, Louis 11
Henry, Alexander 12, 15
Highland Improvement Company 46
Hill, James J. 40
Hjemkomst (ship) 79, 80
Hockey 80
Hoensheller, Emery D. 72
Homecroft School 60
"Honeycomb Class" (cigar
    advertisement) 84, *85*
Hoover, Walter 62
Hopkins, Harry 64
Houghton, Douglass 15
Hoyt, Colgate 43
Hudson Bay 17
Hudson's Bay Company 10, 12, 13
Humphrey, Hubert H. 75
Hunt, William A. 88

I

Ice fishing 80, *93*
Incline railway *46*, 51, 52, *65*, 66
India (ship) 26
Indians 9, *10*, 11, *12*, 14, 15, *16*, *17*,
    21, *22*, *82*, *83*
Ingalls, Edmund *33*
Iron mining 22, 25, 26, 31, 33, 34, 35,
    37, 42, 44, 48, 55, 61, 84
Iron River 55
Ishpeming (dredge) 32
Island Minong 15
Isle Royale 15, 49

J

Jay Cooke and Company 31, 33

Jay Cooke State Park 93
Jefferson School 49
Jeno's Inc. 75
Jesuit Relations (pamphlet) 8
John Fritz (ship) *55*
Johnson, Eastman (artwork of) *12, 82,*
    83
Johnson, George D. 64, 73
Johnson, George W. 68

K

Kay be san day way-we win (Indian)
    12
KDAL 73
Kees, Frederick 55
Kelley-Duluth Hardware 62
Keweenaw Peninsula 15
Kingsbury, W.W. 23
Kitchi Gammi Club 37, 57, 72
Klearfax Linen Looms 67
Knife River 20, 24
Knott, J. Proctor *39*

L

Lady Elgin (steamer) 22, 23
Lake Huron 16
Lake of the Woods 13
Lakeside Land Company 35, 92
Lakeside School 49
Lake Superior 8, 10, 13, 14, 15, 22, *91*,
    92, *95*
Lake Superior and Mississippi
    Railroad 26, *27*, 28, 30, 31
Lake Superior Elevator Company 34
Lake Superior Fish Company 49
Lake Superior Museum of
    Transportation 79
Lake Vermilion 21, 25
Lake Vermilion iron fields 34
Lambert, Eugene 73
La Pointe 12, 14, 16, 17
Lark O' the Lake festival *74*
Lavaque, John *33*
Leif Erikson Park *63*, 79, *90*
Leif Erikson (ship) *63*, 80
Leithead, L.W. 88
LeMasurier, Dalton A. 73
Lemieux, Frank *25*
Lester River 67, 75
Lewis, Ray T. 42, 48
Lewis, Sinclair 63
Lincoln Bank 37
London Road Addition 92
Lovett, Charles E. 45
Luce, Sidney 20, 23, 24, 25, 26, 30
Lyceum Theater 46, *48*, 62, 75

M

McDougall, Alexander 42, *43*, 60
McDougall-Duluth Shipbuilding
    Company 60, *61*
McDougall, Emmeline Ross 43
McKenney, Thomas L. 14, 15
Mackinac Island 21
Mackinac Mission 14
Magney, C.R. 60, 67
"Margaret Culkin Banning Day" 78
Marine Iron and Shipbuilding
    Company 68

Markell, Clinton 38
Marrying (novel) 78
Martin, C.E. 23
Marvin, Luke 25, 26
Mataafa (steamer) 54
Maynard School 53
Meade, George 25
Meinhardt, Anna *49*
Merrill and Ring 48
Merritt, Alfred 10, 24, 31, 48
Merritt family *20*
Merritt, Hephzibah 22
Merritt, Jerome 23
Merritt, L.H. 23
Merritt, Leonidas 47, *66*
Merritt, Lewis *20*, 22, 26, 31
Mesabi hills 21
Mesabi (novel) 78
Middleton 22, 31
Midsummer Festival 79
Milford 23
Miller, A.A. 76
Miller Memorial (Miller-Dwan)
    Hospital 76
Miller, Samuel F. 32
Miller's Creek 37
Minnehaha 53
"Minnehaha" (stained glass window)
    82
Minnesota Air National Guard 72
Minnesota Arrowhead 13, 16, 22, 47,
    64
Minnesota Arrowhead Association 74
Minnesota Canal and Harbor
    Improvement Commission 32
Minnesota Canal Company 54
Minnesota Car Works Company 36,
    42
Minnesota Iron Company 21, 34
Minnesota National Guard 58
Minnesota Point 10, 17, 22, 23, 24, 25,
    27, 30, 31, 32, 36, 42, 51, 54, 73
Minnesota Point lighthouse 18, *19*, 20
Minnesota Point Ship Canal Company
    22
Minnesota Point Street Railway
    Company 36
Minnesota Power and Light Company
    54
Minnesota Steel Company 55, *56*, 59
Minnesota Taconite Amendment 75
Minnesota Third Infantry 58
Minnetonka (train) *79*
Mission Creek Quarry 35
Mitchell and McClure 48
Mitchell, John 13
Mitchell, R.C. 33
Model City 86
Modern Steel Construction Company
    51
Montauk (steamer) 63
Moose Lake 60
Moraski, Bill 72
Morgan and Company, J.P. 41
Morgan, J. Pierpont *41*, 57
Morgan Park 41, *57*
Morrill, James 70
Morrison, William 13, 14
Muhlbaur, Otto 46
Munger, Roger S. 30, 37, 38, 42
Munian, William F. *66*

N

National Football League 62
National Register of Historical Places
    76, 86
National Water Quality Standards
    Laboratory 75
Navy Reserve Seabees (Construction
    Battalion) 72
Nero Duluth Land Company 45, 46
Nettleton, George 8, 17, 18, 22, 23, 24
Nettleton, William *24*
Nevers, Ernie 62
Newspapers: *Duluth Daily News* 35,
    36, 37, 40; *Duluth Herald* 51, 55, 57,
    61, 62, 64, 72; Duluth Herald and
    News-Tribune building *87; Duluth
    Minnesotian* 28, 33; *Duluth News-
    Tribune* 48, 54, 68, 74, 76, 79;
    Duluth Tribune 33, 46; *St. Paul
    Minnesotian* 28
Northern National Bank 66
Northern Pacific Railroad 21, 31, 33,
    34, 45, 79
Northern Steamship line 40
Northland Country Club 60
Northrup, Angeline Peterson *26*
Northrup, Joseph *26*
Northrup, Julia *26*
North Shore Drive *92*
North Star (steamer) 22
Northwest Airways 64
North West Company 13
Northwestern Oil Company *86*
Northwestern Telegraph Company 31
Northwest Passage 10
Norwood, Joseph G. 16
Notin e Garbowik (Eastman Johnson
    painting) 82

O

Oatka Branch *62*
Ojibway Indians *9, 10*, 21
Olav, Crown Prince of Norway 65
Olcott, Chauncey 60
Oliver Iron Mining Company 78
Oneota 21, 22, 23, 35, 36
Oneota Lumber Company 22, 24, 25,
    30
Onsgard, Bert 63
Ontonagon Boulder 15
Ordean Building *45*
Ordean Foundation 45

P

Paine, Frederic W. 88
Palmer, Emmet S. 49
Palmer, Vose 23
Panic of 1837 14
Panic of 1857 24
Park Point *9*, 36, 51, 73, 79
Parks: *52*, 61, 65, 67, 73, 76; Athletic
    Park 64; Canal Park 80, *87*; Cascade
    Park 36, *37, 86*; Chester Park 36, 37;
    Jay Cooke State Park 93; Leif
    Erikson Park *63*, 79, *90*; Morgan
    Park 41, *57*; Spirit Mountain 76, 80,
    90
Paulucci, Jeno F. 75
Pavilion 46, 51, 75
Peabody and Stearns (architects) 86
Peabody, Robert Swain 76

Peet, James 22, 24
People's Brewing 61
Peterson, Peter J. 35
Petroleum 72
Philip, Peter 66
Piedmont Heights 79
Pigeon River 13, 15, 20
Pittsburgh Steel Company 55
Poirier, Camille 30
Pokegama 21
Pokegama Falls 14
Pokegama mission school 14
Police Department 32, 44, 45
Population 24, 28, 32, 33, 35, 45, 68, 72, 74, 77
Port Byron 22
Portland 31
Portland Square 37
Prairie du Chien 14
Prentice, Frederick B. 17, 45
Prince, W. 67
Prindle, William (house of) 88
Prohibition 61, 63, 84

R
Radio 62
Railroads: 26, 27, 28, 40, 61; Bayfield and St. Croix Railroad 39; Canadian Pacific Railroad 34; Duluth and Iron Range Railroad 24, 29, 34, 35, 63, 84, 85; Duluth and Winnipeg Railroad 34; Duluth, Mesabi & Northern Railroad 63; Duluth, Missabe & Iron Range Railroad 39, 63, 70, 71, 84; Duluth, Missabe & Northern Railway 48; Lake Superior and Mississippi Railroad 26, 27, 28, 30, 31; Northern Pacific Railroad 21, 31, 33, 34, 45, 79; St. Paul and Duluth Railroad 34, 35; St. Paul, Minneapolis and Manitoba Railroad 40
Red Cross 60
Red River 17
Refineries 72
Religion 14, 33, 44
Reserve Mining Company 72, 75
Rice, Edmund 22
Rice, Henry 22
Rice, Orrin 22, 23
Rice's Point 22, 23, 31, 32, 35, 42
Robert L. Barnes (ship) 68
Rockefeller, John D. 43, 44, 47
Rogers, W.K. 53
Roman Catholic Diocese of Duluth 44
Roosevelt, Franklin D. 64
Rosenkrantz, C.C. 9
Rudolf, Adolf 53
Russell, Newell F. 89

S
Sacred Heart Church 26
SAGE (semi-automatic ground environment) 77
St. Croix River 11, 39
Saint Germain-Laval 11, 76
St. Lawrence Seaway 74
St. Lawrence Seaway Development Corporation 74
St. Louis Bay 21, 23, 35

St. Louis County Agricultural Society 21
St. Louis County Courthouse 6, 60
St. Louis County Heritage and Arts Center 76
St. Louis County Historical Society 63, 77
St. Louis Hotel Rose Garden 60
St. Louis River 2, 13, 14, 17, 31
St. Luke's Hospital 36, 37
St. Mary's Hospital 36
St. Paul (ship) 31
St. Paul and Duluth Railroad 34, 35
St. Paul, Minneapolis and Manitoba Railroad 40
St. Paul Minnesotian (newspaper) 28
Salisbury, Frank 25
Salsich, LeRoy 78
Salter School 49
Sargent, George B. 17, 27, 30, 33
Sault Ste. Marie 10, 14, 16, 42
Schiller-Hubbard Company 34
Schoolcraft, Henry Rowe 14
Schools: 36, 47; Central High School 47, 49, 86; Cobb School 60; Craggencroft School 53; Duluth Normal School 47, 53, 70; Hardy School 53; Homecroft School 60; Jefferson School 49; Lakeside School 49; Maynard School 53; Salter School 49; Washington Junior High School 49
Schultz, August 61
Schultz, Henry 61
Seaway Port Authority 74, 77
Sellwood, Joseph 55; (house of) 88
Sellwood, Othelia 88
Sellwood, Richard 55
Seven Years' War 12
Shefchik, Thomas J. 6
Ship Canal 23, 35
Shipping 22, 23, 31, 43, 61, 68, 69, 72, 73, 74, 91
Shoenberger, John H. 33
Sieur du Lhut Room (St. Louis County Historical Society) 83
Silver Broom Competition 90
Sioux Indians 10, 11, 12, 14
Sisters of St. Benedict 36, 47
Skyline Boulevard 67
Skyline Drive 37, 46
Skyline Parkway 53, 80
Slack, Kay 77
Smith, James, Jr. 27
Smith, Vespasian 33
Snively Parkway 67
Snively, Samuel F. 65, 66, 67
Society of Jesus 73
Soo Locks 20, 73
Spalding Hotel 45, 46, 75
Spalding, William 45
Spanish American War 50
Spanish influenza epidemic 60
Spencer, George 33, 44
Spirit Lake 45
Spirit Mountain 76, 80, 90
Sports 46, 47, 62
Statue of Liberty replica 47
Stearns, John Goddard 76
Stearns, O.P. 33
Steel Trust 55

Stone, George C. 21, 30
Stone-Ordean-Wells 45; (advertisement) 85
Stone's Bank 30
Strike of 1889 44, 45
Stuntz, George 16, 17, 18, 20, 21, 26, 30, 34
Sunrise Terrace farm 88
Superior City 8, 16, 17, 18, 20, 22
Sutphin, John B. 37, 44
Swedish Midsummer Festival 79

T
Taconite 71, 72
Telegraph 30
Television 73
Ten Eyck, James E. 63
Terrace Drive 38
Thomas W. Lamont (ore boat) 95
Thomas Wilson (whaleback) 43
Thompson Junction 31
Thomson Dam 54
Thomson, Robert B. 66
Tiffany, Louis C. 82
Tikinagan (cradle board) 83
Timber industry 22, 23, 25, 28, 31, 35, 37, 46, 48, 74, 93
Torrey Building 47
Tourism 74, 75, 76, 77, 79, 80
Tower, Charlemagne 34
Tower, Charlemagne, Jr. 29, 34
Traphagen, Oliver 44
Treaty of La Pointe, 1854, signing of, 16, 26
Treaty of Fond du Lac 14
Truman, Harry 68
Trysil Ski Club 47
Twain, Mark 80
Twin Ports 25, 32
Two Harbors 24, 35
Typhoid epidemic (1882, 1888) 36

U
U.S.-Canadian St. Lawrence Seaway 73, 74
U.S. Life Savers 54
U.S. Steel Corporation 41, 55, 57, 59, 76
U.S. Steel Duluth Works 60, 66
Ulland, Laurel 88
Ulland Restoration Project 88
Union Depot 47, 76, 77, 79, 80, 86
Union Improvement and Elevator Company 30
Unions 75
United States Indian Department 14
Universal Portland Cement Company 60
University of Minnesota-Duluth 47, 70, 72, 75, 76, 79

V
Van Brunt, Walter (fireman) 33
Van Brunt, Walter (historian) 58
Vecchi, Thomas A. (house of) 92
Vermilion and Mesabi Range 56
Vermilion Range 24
Vermilion Trail 26, 34
Villa, Pancho 58
Villa St. Scholastica 53

W
Walleye (state fish) 93
War of 1812 13
Washburn, Genevieve (house of) 89
Washburn, Jed L. 67, 89
Washington Junior High School 49
Watrous, John 23
Welland Canal 73
West Duluth 36
West Duluth Blast Furnace Company 55, 56
Western Land Association 30, 45
Weston, Anne Vanderlip 82
Weston, J.B. 53
Whaleback 43, 44
Wheeler, H.W. 22
Wigemar Wasung (Indian) 12
Williams and Company, W.W. 32
Williams, John G. 67
Williamson-Johnson Municipal Airport 64
Wilson, Joseph 8, 17, 73
Wisted, David Gilbert 61
WJAP 62
Wolvin, A.B. 55
Woolson, Albert 73
Work People's College 53
Works Progress Administration (WPA) 64, 65, 73
Work Projects Administration Writers' Program 73
World War I 58, 60, 61, 85
World War II 68, 69, 72

Y
Young Men's Christian Association 33

Z
Zenith Furnace Company 56

PARTNERS IN PROGRESS
Arrowhead Hearing Aid Center 109
Clyde Iron 104, 105
Como Oil Company 113
Crawford Funeral Service 120
Diamond Tool and Horseshoe Co. 118
Duluth, Winnipeg & Pacific Railroad 101
First Bank-Duluth 99
Industrial Weldors & Machinists, Inc. 123
Johnson Mortuary 119
Kemp Fisheries, Inc., A. 117
Lake Haven Manor 115
M&K Stores 112
McLennan Company, S.A. 108
Main Hurdman 111
Marine Iron and Ship Building Company 110
Miller-Dwan Medical Center 121
Minnesota Power 100
Pioneer National Bank of Duluth 122
Radisson Hotel Corporation 124
Reach-All Manufacturing and Engineering Inc. 103
St. Louis County Historical Society 98
St. Luke's Hospital 116
St. Mary's Hospital 102
Superwood Corporation 107
WEBC Radio 114
Zenith Dredge Company 106